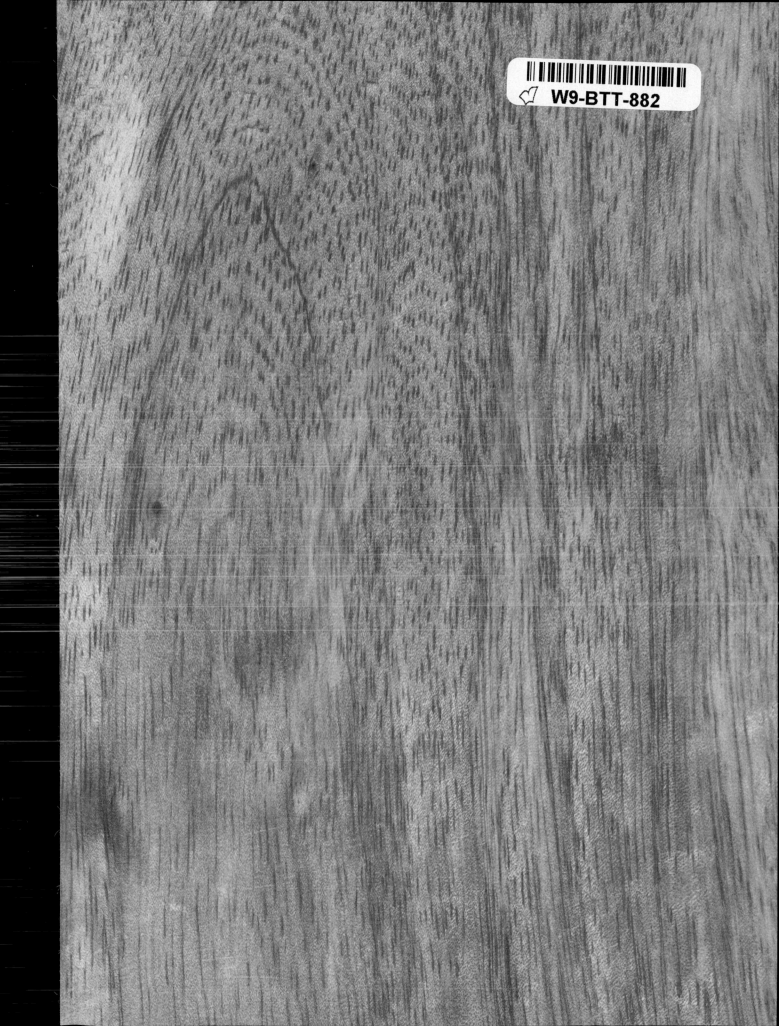

ON BOARDS

ON BOARDS

SIMPLE & INSPIRING
RECIPE IDEAS TO SHARE
AT EVERY GATHERING

LISA DAWN BOLTON

appetite
by RANDOM HOUSE

Appetite by Random House® and colophon are registered trademarks of Penguin Random House LLC.

Library and Archives of Canada Cataloguing in Publication is available upon request.
ISBN: 978-0-14-753114-8
eBook ISBN: 978-0-14-753115-5

Cover and book design: Jennifer Griffiths
Cover and book photography: Lisa Dawn Bolton; (marble) © Prasit Jamkajornkiat / EyeEm / Getty Images
Photography on pages 28, 29, 66, 67, 84, 85, 106, 107 and 181 by Janis Nicolay
Printed and bound in China

Published in Canada by Appetite by Random House®,
a division of Penguin Random House Canada Limited.

www.penguinrandomhouse.ca

10 9 8 7 6

appetite
by RANDOM HOUSE | Penguin
Random House
Canada

Mom and Dad, for a lifetime of love
and encouragement.

Rick, forever my favorite person on
the other side of any board.

Matteo, my most beautiful creation.

Contents

The Boards

The Recipes

Introduction

Welcome! Come in, pull up a cushion (yes, cushion) and sit down. Make yourself comfortable, and let me tell you a little about how I love to eat.

When I recall my fondest food memories, they're filled with people sharing simple food, family-style. People crowded around a table, passing bites around. People curled up with their feet on the sofa, wineglass perched delicately on the armrest. People sitting on cushions eating casually, no utensils required. And I'm not off fussing in the kitchen; I'm with everyone else, enjoying every last bite of baguette, Brie and blackberry, not giving a second thought to anything other than the moment. If that sounds like an experience you would like to be a part of, this book is for you, because that's the beauty of a big, bountiful board, a board full of food to pick and share from. Because of that board, I don't have to be stressing over dinner—I can sit back and enjoy the company of my family and friends. For me, the recipe for a perfect gathering is:

Find some good company.
Gather around a big board.
Make some great memories.

I truly believe you don't have to prep and plan an elaborate spread every time you want to entertain. The effort that goes into hosting shouldn't overshadow what you serve. But the pressure we put on ourselves can be overwhelming. Trust me, I've been there. Anticipating guests on the weekend, scouring my cookbooks for that perfect dish, making four stops to gather every item in a long list of ingredients. Then, after following the recipe to the letter, closing the oven door and just praying it works. Only for when the guests finally arrive, to still be too busy in the kitchen to actually spend time with them! That used to be me. But not anymore. It was when I had a family of my own that I realized how fast time passes and that the little moments in life are what really matter. I didn't want to miss those moments because I was too busy whisking a sauce to hear the stories being shared in the other room.

Serving food on boards is the perfect solution to serving something delicious that has also, almost entirely, been prepared in advance. Most of what goes onto a board can be made ahead of time, so you never have the stress of timing a perfect meal. And the best thing about boards is that no matter your culinary skill level, you can create something beautiful. But no matter how the board turns out, it will be the stories, laughter and company that people will remember. Whether you're having a picnic with close friends or a fabulous New Year's Eve celebration, boards are really about the people sitting around them and give you a real chance to eat, share and connect with those you love.

HOW TO USE THIS BOOK

On Boards is not a cookbook in the traditional sense. It's more of a book of inspiration broken into three parts. Part one provides information on getting started: types of boards and serving tools, types and amounts of ingredients, and tips on arrangement and presentation. Part two contains the stars of the show, the boards: 50 ideas for all seasons and occasions. Part three features the recipes: 52 simple dips, sauces and other tasty additions to make ahead of time and serve as part of your boards.

Part one offers advice to help you build the very best boards. This is not a cheese education book or a charcuterie book, so you won't find history lessons or steps for how to make your own. You *will* find an introduction to some cheese varietals and pairings and some types of meat that you may not have encountered before. If you've never had a cheese board for dessert, I suspect you'll be pleasantly surprised. And blue cheese paired with smoked mussels? Who knew?!

When you turn to part two, you'll find it looks a little different from most cookbooks. For each board, I have listed components rather than ingredients, followed by short, simple prep information where required, rather than a detailed step-by-step method (so, you'll notice that sometimes not every component appears in the prep section).

The components are listed in the way I hope will be most useful to you when preparing your boards. First are any recipes that appear in the book, as these can be prepared in advance. Then come fresh fruits and vegetables, as they usually require the most prep work on the day. Meats, fish and cheeses come next, followed by breads and crackers, accompaniments (like pickles, preserves or nuts) and finally garnishes, which are always optional.

All quantities for the components are approximate. If a board calls for eight carrots, this is just a guideline. Unlike when you're making carrot

DRINK SUGGESTIONS

For some boards, I offer an idea about the type(s) of drinks to serve alongside. These aren't meant to be "pairings" in the official sense. I fully subscribe to the philosophy that the best wine for the dish is the one that's already open! I love wine, all wine—cheap and cheerful or rich and fancy. But I have discovered some things to avoid when it comes to pairing: smoked fish and red wine is one of them (these are very difficult to consume together without their both tasting off). I've also found some that are matches made in heaven: asparagus and Brussels sprouts are hard to eat with anything other than a crisp, cold Sauvignon Blanc, and strong blue cheeses usually need the brute force of a sweet Port. The recommended pairings aren't necessarily wine, but just those that I believe will enhance the food and the theme of the board overall.

cake, for example, adding more or fewer carrots to a board will not ruin the end result. And while I suggest a certain weight for meats and cheeses, I should also admit that after creating quite literally hundreds of boards, I still have a hard time visualizing what 4 ounces of prosciutto looks like! I also know that "thinly sliced" can be interpreted very differently at a speciality deli and a corner-store grocer. So again, weights are for guidance only and not to be followed precisely. Each board has a suggested serving size, which I've based on the board being enjoyed as an "opening act" (see page 11 to understand what I mean by that!), but it's just that: a suggestion.

On Boards is designed to be an inspiration for home entertaining. It should encourage you to try new meats, cheeses, fruits and vegetables and new ways of presenting and serving them. As you create boards from this book, don't get tied down trying to make them exactly as described or as shown in the photos. Instead, consider the boards in this book as a jumping-off point. Let your local market be your guide; judge the quality of the produce in front of you and substitute as necessary. Don't select subpar produce simply to match what you see in the book—taste should always reign supreme! Do what feels best for you, and have the confidence that you can create a beautiful spread for any occasion.

Begin

TYPES OF BOARDS

Boards are readily available to buy almost every where these days, from grocery stores to bookstores to home stores. I prefer boards made from natural materials, like wood, marble and slate, because I believe food from nature looks its best on natural surfaces. Of course, almost all of the boards in this book could be served on glass, porcelain plates or even plastic trays if that's what you have at hand. It's really the quality of the ingredients and how you present them that matter most.

I recommend you start your board collection with three wooden boards: a round one, a long rectangular one and one with a rimmed edge, all of slightly different sizes and hues. The best sizes for you will depend on the gatherings you tend to have. I have a small family and we live in a relatively small space, but I still enjoy the grandiose feel of a large board. My go-to board for more intimate gatherings measures 11″ × 16″, has a dark hue and has brilliant white handles that make transporting it a breeze. For larger spreads, consider something closer to 20″ × 13″ in a tray format (to make it easier to carry). You could also consider investing in two smaller boards if you tend to have guests with dietary restrictions; for example, you could keep one board for strict vegans or guests with nut allergies.

WOODEN BOARDS

Most of the boards I initially created were on my old wooden cutting board. Over the years, I've built a hefty—quite literally—collection of wooden boards in every shape, size and color, yet I mainly use the same five or six boards. If you care for your wooden board properly, it should last for years.

Some food, such as cheese, tends to pick up the flavors of softwood boards (such as oak, pine, cedar and fir), so look for hardwoods like maple, teak, birch and olive instead.

CARE

TO CLEAN: Sprinkle both sides of the board with coarse salt, rub with half of a lemon, rinse well with hot water and dry immediately; or simply wash the board well on both sides in warm, soapy water and use a bristle brush to ensure any cracks are well cleaned out. Sometimes highly pigmented foods like berries can leave stains on your wooden boards.

TO REMOVE STAINS: Sprinkle the affected area with coarse sea salt. Cut a lemon in half, squeeze the lemon juice over the salt and then use the flesh side of the lemon to rub the lemon juice and salt into the stain. Finally, add a small amount of baking soda. Rub the area with a damp cloth, rinse and let dry.

TO OIL: When you purchase a wooden board, and about every ten uses afterward, oil both sides with a food-grade oil such as almond, walnut, coconut or mineral oil, or with spoon oil—a mixture of beeswax and mineral oil. Mineral oil is sold at home improvement stores that carry lumber, most home décor stores and pharmacies. If you use a nut-based oil, don't serve food on that board to anyone with a nut allergy.

TO PREVENT WARPING: Never soak a wooden board, and always apply the same treatment to both sides.

SLATE BOARDS

Slate is one of the most durable naturally occurring stones, and thanks to its increase in popularity, it's reasonably priced and readily available at most home and kitchen stores. It's also nonporous and nonreactive, making it quite resistant to smells and stains and less prone to discoloration.

Slate found at tiling and home improvement stores may be dyed or porous and tend to flake. Ask the retailer if the slate is food-safe. If they can't confirm it is, it's safer to assume it's not. Kitchen slate sold in home stores is predominantly black (not dyed) and is usually food-safe. Its dark color makes it a beautiful backdrop—it's gorgeous with white cheeses and red and purple cured meats—and you can use chalk or soapstone to write on it. As well, slate can cope with extreme hot and cold temperatures, so you can use a slate board as a trivet for hot pots or freeze it before you plate to keep everything cool if serving your board outside on a hot day.

Unfortunately, slate tends to scratch and scuff easily. You can try to buff out any marks with a non-abrasive substance such as baking soda, or just

MAKE YOUR OWN FOOD-SAFE BOARDS

Unfortunately, you can't just take any old piece of wood and turn it into a serving platter. Boards with a lacquer finish or varnish are not guaranteed to be food-safe (and neither are the ceramic, slate and granite tiles at your local home improvement store). But if you have access to natural hardwood stumps or limbs that have been dried and seasoned, you can definitely try making your own board. (You can also buy hardwood slices at craft stores or online.)

Untreated wood can be made food-safe in three steps: cleaning, sanding, then oiling. To clean the board, use a dry stiff-bristled brush to clear the surface and surrounding bark of any debris or moss that could come in contact with food. Then sand the surface, first with a 150-grit paper and then with a 220-grit paper. Next, oil the board. Use a clean, dry cloth to apply a generous coating of mineral oil in the direction of the grain. Untreated wood will soak up a lot of oil on the first application, so plan for several coats, leaving at least an hour between coats. I recommend doing two coats the first day, leaving the board overnight and applying a third coat in the morning. Wipe off any excess oil in the morning.

embrace the nicks and use them to recall the memories of a great night.

CARE

TO CLEAN: Hand-wash with warm, soapy water, rinse with hot water and dry thoroughly.

TO REMOVE STAINS: Rub with a soft cloth and food-safe mineral oil.

TO OIL: Once or twice a year, rub a few drops of mineral oil into the board to preserve its luster, give it a nice shine and prevent food from sticking to or staining it.

MARBLE BOARDS

A beautiful contrast to the dark tone of slate, marble is another natural surface perfect for serving food. The crisp, cool tone of marble exudes elegance and makes the colors of fruits and vegetables pop. Marble boards can be purchased as single pieces, but they're also quite commonly found as combination wood/marble boards. Because marble is naturally cool, it's ideal if you're serving cheeses and meats or hosting an outdoor event. It doesn't absorb smells or stains as easily as wood, so it's the ideal platter for a stinky blue. You can also write on it if you have a charcoal pen.

Marble is prone to etching from acidic foods such as tomatoes or lemons and pigmented liquids such as red wine, so if you're serving these on marble, either cover the board with parchment paper or rinse and wash it immediately after use. Finally, never use a marble board as a cutting board. It will wreck the board and your knives.

CARE

TO CLEAN: Hand-wash with mild soapy, warm water and dry immediately. Avoid acidic cleaners (vinegar or lemon juice, for example), as they can erode the board.

TO REMOVE STAINS: Apply a thick paste of flour and water to the stain, cover the board with plastic wrap for up to 48 hours and then wipe the paste away. You may need to repeat this process.

SERVING TOOLS

CHARCUTERIE TOOLS

Charcuterie comes in three basic formats: whole (like a salami link), sliced (like prosciutto) or spreadable (like pâté). While you may have to buy specialty cheese knives, a charcuterie-tool set is pretty easy to assemble from standard kitchen tools (and cheese knives).

CHARCUTERIE KNIFE: I usually prefer to serve cured hard salamis in their whole form. I slice off a few pieces to get my guests started, then let people cut their own. A sharp cheese cleaver or spade works great here. It's sharp enough to cut through the casing, but small enough to sit unobtrusively on or near the board. You can also use a thin, very delicate paring or steak knife. The smaller and sharper the better.

CHARCUTERIE FORK: Small, slim forks are great for picking up pieces of thinly sliced meats. I often use a lobster fork.

CHARCUTERIE SPREADER: The best way to serve spreadable charcuterie is with a spreader. It's perfect for scooping out the ideal serving of rillettes or gliding through a block of pâté. If your cheese-knife set contains a spreader, decide if you want to use it for only cheese or charcuterie. This will help avoid possible cross-contamination, which is important if guests have allergies or specific diets.

CHEESE TOOLS

Cheese comes in many shapes and sizes, and so do cheese knives. While I'm not usually a stickler for the rules, I recommend you invest in a small cheese-knife set. If you're going to go to the trouble of creating a beautiful board, it deserves more than a steak knife stuck in the Gouda! For under $20, you can get a basic four-piece knife set that will get you through most boards. And if you feel like really indulging, consider adding a spreader and planer (see below).

PRONGED CHEESE KNIFE: This multi-purpose knife is sharp enough to cut through a semifirm cheese or rind but has a small-enough surface area to prevent the cheese from sticking. The prongs on the end can be used to serve cheese or crumble off a hard varietal. If you buy only one cheese knife, this should be it. And buy two.

CHEESE CLEAVER/SPADE: The cleaver looks just like a mini meat cleaver; the spade resembles half a heart. Both are used for slicing into hard and firm cheeses.

CHEESE FORK: This looks like a pitchfork. Its sole purpose is to serve sliced cheese.

SOFT-CHEESE KNIFE: This is the sharp, often serrated knife with holes in the blade. The knife is sharp enough to cut through rind, but the holes prevent the soft, creamy cheese inside from sticking to the blade.

SPREADER: This knife is rounded with a blade no sharper than a butter knife's and is used for spreadable cheeses. Spreaders are also wide enough to get just the right-size dollop of cream cheese and the perfect schmear of hummus, dip or spread.

CHEESE PLANER: This is my fancy-pants cheese knife. Drag it across a Fontina, Havarti or Gouda—or any semifirm cheese—to shave off the perfect slice.

FRUIT & VEGETABLE TOOLS

The beauty of investing in tools for cutting fruits and vegetables is that you'll be able to use them regularly in your kitchen for everyday meals. Whether you're making zucchini noodles or scalloped potatoes, these tools not only produce beautiful cuts for boards, but will speed up your prep time.

SWIVEL OR Y PEELER: A peeler is so much more than a tool to remove vegetable skins. It's a fun way to cut and serve vegetables as well. I use a peeler to create beautiful ribbons of asparagus, carrot and cucumber. The swivel peeler's blade pivots as it moves across the fruit or vegetable. The Y peeler's blade almost pivots, but instead of pushing it away, you draw it toward you. I prefer the Y peeler as it gives me more control.

JULIENNE PEELER: Shaped like either a swivel peeler or Y peeler, this has a serrated blade that creates fine strands of the fruit or vegetable as you peel. It makes perfectly uniform strips and works best on hard fruits and vegetables. (Try it on root vegetables like kohlrabi, beets or carrots.)

SPIRALIZER: This inexpensive tool is about the size of a toaster and turns fresh fruits and vegetables into long, noodle-like strands. Like a peeler, it works best on firm produce like apples or carrots, but you can also use it on zucchini for an alternative to pasta.

MANDOLINE: I saved the best for last. This is by far my most beloved fruit and vegetable tool. I feared the mandoline for many years, but now use mine almost daily. There's no faster way to get perfectly uniform slices. Most mandolines come with blades that allow you to julienne and waffle-cut as well. But be careful: the blade is sharp. Always use the guard.

OTHER TOOLS

There are a few other easy-to-find tools that will make diving into a board easier for your guests.

SPOONS: You can never have enough small spoons. I love to scour thrift shops for old collectible teaspoons about 4″ long and made from wood, glass, copper or silver. They work perfectly for small dishes of preserves, sauces or seeds.

TONGS: I have about half a dozen pairs of miniature tongs. I set them directly on the board or put several on a small plate next to the board. They're perfect for picking up slices of meat or sausage and make it easier to grasp vegetables like green string beans.

TOOTHPICKS: Stick a handful of plain or decorative toothpicks in a dish of olives, or nuzzle them in a crevice between some meats on the

board. They act as personal serving tools, with the added bonus of being disposable. Just remember to avoid the flavored ones unless you want your olives minty fresh!

SMALL BOWLS AND PLATES: Sometimes the components of a board benefit from separation. Small matte dishes and bowls are more treasures I seek out in home stores and thrift stores—they work great for nuts, olives, preserves and spreads. Most of my bowls are 2″ to 4″ in diameter and no taller than 2″.

HIMALAYAN SALT BLOCK: This may soon become your most coveted kitchen tool. Not only does it make a beautiful serving vessel, but you can cook, bake and cure on it. There are whole cookbooks dedicated to cooking with salt blocks! For boards, I love them as a vessel to keep seafood really cold and add just a hint of salt. ■

Gather

HOW MUCH DO I NEED?

This is the most common question I am asked about boards. To determine the answer, first you have to ask the question: What role will the board play?

THE OPENING ACT

This board is a small appetizer before a big meal. It's the board that's out as guests arrive, offering a little something to whet their appetite, but not satisfy their hunger. For this board, everything is scaled back: one to two slices of meat or cheese per person, one to two tablespoons of spread and two to three vegetables or accompaniments. This board also works for a late-night nibble with drinks when you have guests over after dinner.

THE ENSEMBLE

This board is part of a bigger cast. It's part of a pot-luck where it's not intended to feed everyone. It could also be a board you're serving at home alongside a few hot canapés. It needs to be heartier than the opening act, but isn't expected to satisfy the appetite of every guest on its own.

THE STAR

This board is the meal. This is where you want to go all out and make sure you have enough selection and quantity to thoroughly satisfy your guests. Envision someone filling a dinner plate from the board and calculate your portions from there. It's a good idea to hold back some prepped components like cut vegetables or sliced meat and replenish the board when required.

Once you know what role your board is playing, you can think about the other variables that may alter how much of everything you need. For example, what's the ratio of adults to children? Are any of your guests known for having a large appetite? If you don't know the makeup of the crowd, just treat every adult as a serving. In this book, my suggested serving sizes are for four or eight people when the board is meant to be the opening act, but note I always tend to have too much rather than too little!

MEAT & CHEESE

Most people recommend a certain number of ounces per person for meat and cheese. While this can be a good starting point, I also take into account the following:

1 *Variation in richness and flavor:* When it comes to blue cheese, less is more. I wouldn't treat it the same way I would a crowd-friendly Gouda, for example. The same applies to meat. I'd serve less of an exotic pâté or very spicy salami than I would something lighter and milder.

2 *Number of slices is easier:* It's difficult to visualize ounces when it comes to meat and cheese, and much easier to ballpark slices or servings. Depending on the role the board is playing, I estimate how many slices of meat each guest will have and then multiply by the number of guests. That said, quite often salamis, for example, are sold in whole rings and by weight only, so on some of the boards you will see quantity expressed in ounces if that makes more sense for buying purposes. I also consider things like the number of vegetarians who'll be joining us.

FRUITS & VEGETABLES

Err on the side of more for fruit and vegetables, for two reasons. First, these are the most cost-effective parts of your board. A few extra radishes or carrots will not break the bank. Second, vegetables are part of our everyday diet, so they're easier to use up as leftovers than something like liver pâté.

BREAD & CRACKERS

You can't beat the price of a baguette. Even if I'm going with crackers on a board, I always have an extra baguette on hand just in case. For a dollar or two, you can soak up a lot of dip (or alcohol), and even if it's a bit crusty the next day, you can use it to make bread crumbs.

ACCOMPANIMENTS

Calculating how much dip you need is more of an art than a science. I allocate about 3 tablespoons of dip per person for a three-hour evening. If you're hosting ten people, put at least a 2-cup serving on the board and have at least 1 cup on reserve.

Nuts, olives, pickles and dried fruits are readily available in bulk, which makes it easier to get the portion sizes you need. Usually these are meant to just enhance the board, and a little will go a long

way. The upside? Most of these extras have long shelf lives.

CHARCUTERIE: TYPES, SLICING & SERVING

Pronounced shar-koo-ter-ee, *this intimidating word has evolved in its interpretation (and spelling) over the years. It comes from the French word* chaircuiterie *(*chair *= flesh;* cuit *= cooked).*

TYPES OF CHARCUTERIE

In North America, charcuterie has become a catch-all word that can be loosely divided into three categories: cured sausages, whole muscle cuts and pâtés, terrines and rillettes.

CURED SAUSAGES: Fat and meat, most often pork, are finely minced and stuffed into a casing. From there, they are cured by being packed in salt, smoked or air-dried. The most popular types of cured sausages are hard salamis like saucisson or pepperoni.

WHOLE MUSCLE CUTS: The fat and meat are still intact as they would be on the animal. Some of the more popular whole muscle cuts are prosciutto, speck, capocollo and bresaola. When sliced thin, they have an almost silky texture and a blast of salty, savory flavor. These popular meats are made by covering the muscle (most often the leg) with salt and spice and hanging it to dry in a controlled, cold environment for about 12 months, depending on the type of ham. Ever wonder why prosciutto di Parma is so much more expensive than other prosciuttos or cured hams? It's all in the curing process. The finest pigs from Parma, Italy, are raised on a diet that includes the whey from Parmigiano-Reggiano, and the final product is preservative-free. The sweeter, smoother taste this produces is always branded with a five-star crown seal of approval from the Parma Ham Consortium.

PÂTÉS, TERRINES AND RILLETTES: Pâté is a finely ground mixture of meat, fat and spices plus textural elements such as nuts or vegetables. A terrine is similar, but can contain other things like pastry or vegetables and is layered and cooked in a loaf-style pan. A rillette is animal protein that has been shredded or roughly chopped and confited in its own fat. A rillette has more texture than a pâté or terrine and can be found on menus as potted pork.

HOW TO SLICE CHARCUTERIE

Cured meats are purchased either whole or sliced. The diameter of the sausage and how much you need will determine whether you serve it whole or sliced. I prefer to serve sausages whole on a board when they're smaller than about 2″ in diameter. This reduces the meat's exposure to air, keeping it fresher longer. If the sausage is larger than 2″ in diameter and you're purchasing it whole, slice it cold and serve it at room temperature. The meat is firmer when it's cold, making it easier to get your desired thickness.

If you're slicing charcuterie at home, select a 10″ to 12″ knife that's thin in gauge, narrow and extremely sharp. This will give you the most control and allow you to shave very thin slices if desired. I like to cut salami on the bias for a more oblong shape, but it's up to you. Slicing a hard salami about ¼″ thick or less is ideal because it tends to be quite toothsome, and any thicker can feel more like a jerky texture. The meat package will indicate if the rind is edible; *most* salamis from speciality butchers have edible rinds, but if in doubt, either peel the rind away or ensure your guests know to do so.

Slices ordered from a delicatessen can be thick, thin or shaved. It's usually best to order the meat sliced thin. For a more expensive salami, ask for a very thin, almost shaved slice. The rich and potent flavor means a little will go a long way, and thin slices will let you stretch the number you can get out of an order.

Whole muscle cuts like ham or prepared meats like pastrami should be cut as thin as possible without being shaved. The slice should be intact, but you should almost be able to see through it. This makes it easy to pick up, but not too thick and overpowering when placed on a crostini or cracker.

HOW TO SERVE CHARCUTERIE

Place each slice of cured meat individually on the board. If the meat has been sliced at the butcher, don't just transfer the fanned-out slices from the butcher paper to the board. After being wrapped up and compressed, the slices tend to stick together, meaning your guests will have to separate them out.

With larger salamis, fold the individual slices over slightly so they're easy to pick up; their shape will also create a nice element of height on the board. Whole muscle cuts should be draped onto the board, one slice at a time, into small piles. For more tips on how to serve charcuterie, see page 7.

CHEESE: TYPES, SLICING & SERVING

My approach to cheese is much like my approach to wine. I'm open to trying anything once, often twice. There are many beautiful, delectable cheeses in the world, and you might find you're pleasantly surprised by what you discover. Life is short. Try the cheese.

TYPES OF CHEESE

Cheese can be broken into so many categories—type of milk, rind, texture, flavor, age and on it goes. It can all be a bit overwhelming, so to keep it simple, I break cheese into six basic types:

FRESH: This is young, soft, rindless cheese. The high water content makes many varietals almost

spreadable, and some types have a tangy or sour profile. Try ricotta, burrata or Feta.

BLOOMY RIND: This creamy cheese has an edible rind that forms when the cheese is exposed to a specific type of mold. It is usually white and takes on an earthy, mushroom flavor. Try Brie or Camembert.

SEMISOFT: A creamy, sliceable cheese whose rind is usually not edible. Cheeses in this category are what I call your "safe for a crowd" varieties. Try Havarti, fontina or Monterey Jack.

FIRM/HARD: This very broad category of cheese ranges from very mild (think Swiss) to sharp and pungent (think aged Asiago), and from grateable

to elastic. Most often there is a natural rind that is edible but sometimes not palatable. Try Cheddar, Gruyère or Parmesan.

BLUE CHEESE: And then there's blue. Blue is one of the most divisive cheeses I know of. Technically semisoft, it has a not-quite-accurate reputation for being strong and pungent. Two different strains of mold are used to make blue cheese—*Penicillium roqueforti* and *Penicillium glaucum*—and these influence its flavor and strength. The former is the magic behind the strong-tasting Roquefort; the latter produces a much milder, nuttier cheese, such as bleu d'Auvergne. I try to isolate the blue a little on a board, and I flank it with sweet flavors like honey or grapes or a vehicle such as a cracker or crostini. If you want to convert your blue-despising friends, try an Italian Gorgonzola dolce or Spanish Monte Enebro (technically a goat cheese encased in mold).

GOAT CHEESE: Goat cheese gets its own category because, like blue, it's another polarizing cheese. Most people associate it with chèvre—the white, soft but sort of crumbly, fairly spreadable cheese most commonly sold in a log shape—but goat cheese is so much more than that. Try the Californian Humboldt Fog chèvre from Cypress Grove, the Spanish Drunken Goat (semifirm) or an aged goat Gouda (firm).

HOW TO SLICE CHEESE

Delicious cheese cut incorrectly is still delicious cheese. But with all the different shapes of cheese out there, it's helpful to know how to dig in, especially for that first slice. The key word here is slice. Never saw the cheese; cut it evenly in one fluid motion.

The diagram on page 15 shows you all the different ways to cut a block of cheese. On a board, it's nice to cut off a few slices to get your guests started. (See page 8 for the types of knives to use for different types of cheese.)

HOW TO SERVE CHEESE

The golden rule of serving cheese: don't serve it cold. Cheese is a living organism, closely linked with fermentation. A bit of warmth will highlight any umami flavor you're hoping to experience, so remove cheese from the refrigerator 30 to 60 minutes prior to serving. When possible, don't slice cheese until you're ready to serve it. As soon as it's sliced, it starts to lose some of its aroma and flavor.

Finally, try to avoid having cheeses touch each other. Slices from the same cheese can overlap, but different cheeses can take on each other's characteristics. And as in the famous "Farmer in the Dell" nursery rhyme, the blue cheese stands alone. Always. For more tips on how to serve cheese, see page 8.

FRUITS & VEGETABLES

If meat and cheese are the foundations of a board, fruits and vegetables are what bring it to life. Vibrant, colorful, seasonal produce catches the eye and draws people in. It adds a balance of texture and color when interspersed with the processed components (meat, cheese, pickles or preserves) and gives the palate a cleansing rest stop between these richer elements.

That doesn't mean that fruits and vegetables can't be used alone for a board; if you make careful choices about which ones to present or the way you present them, they can be the stars! I bet most people won't even miss the meat and cheese on the Vegan Vibes board (page 58).

Fruits and vegetables are also an inexpensive way to add bulk to your boards. And you don't have to worry about having one of everything for everybody (unless the board is for children, as they're not always the most gracious sharers!).

HOW TO SLICE & SERVE FRUITS

My first piece of advice on cutting fruit is that in many cases, you shouldn't. Many fruits—for example, small stone fruits like apricots and plums, or a perfect pear or satsuma orange with the stem and leaf still attached—are great to add to a board whole as edible garnishes.

If you do slice the fruit, experiment with different ways of styling it. Use a mandoline to shave off ribbons of cantaloupe or thin, even slices of apple. Slice watermelon into sticks instead of wedges. Exotic fruits like papaya or dragon fruit need only be sliced in half to become works of art. And you can make beautiful skewers of assorted berries using toothpicks.

Fruits like apples and pears oxidize quickly once exposed to air so they should be stored in lemon water (five parts water to one part lemon juice) until you need them. For berries, wash them just prior to using and gently pat dry.

HOW TO SLICE & SERVE VEGETABLES

Walk into any supermarket deli and you're sure to find a veggie tray with celery sticks, cucumber coins and mechanically peeled baby carrots. While there's absolutely nothing wrong with this, I think you're ready to take your veggie game to the next level. I hope that after reading *On Boards*, you'll leave the leaves on your celery sticks, make ribbons out of cucumbers and ditch the pasty orange nubs for bushy green-topped carrots plucked right from the field!

The good news is that veggies need minimal prep for using on boards. Celery, for example, is the ultimate dipper. Its natural hollow makes it the ideal vessel for a scoop of hummus or a schmear of cream cheese, and it naturally grows in different lengths, so I believe it's perfectly okay to display them that way on a board. Cucumbers can be cut into coins and sticks, of course, but try shaving them into ribbons or hollow them out to hold dips. A small bunch of carrots needs only to be lightly scrubbed and left with about 2″ of greens to become beautiful and interesting, rather than lifeless and dull. (This applies to radishes too.) Use your imagination!

When preparing boards ahead of time, store hard vegetables in water in the refrigerator. When ready to use, remove them from the water, pat dry and add to the board.

Some vegetables become more palatable after a quick blanch—the technique of dropping vegetables into a pot of boiling water for 1 to 2 minutes, then into an ice bath to stop the cooking process. This not only takes the harsh bite out of certain vegetables (just a minute in the water can make all the difference for broccoli), it also brings out the vibrant colors of others (green string beans and asparagus, for example).

BREAD & CRACKERS

If the bun makes the burger, bread and crackers make the board! Whether you choose bread, crackers or both, every board needs a reliable vehicle for that spicy salami, pungent cheese or creamy dip.

BREAD

You can't go wrong with a crusty French baguette. You can slice it up or leave it whole and have your guests tear into it. Served fresh, it is perfect for dipping into oil and vinegar or melty fondue cheese. A baguette is also perfect for crostini (see Crostini for a Crowd on page 47): sliced thin, drizzled with oil and popped under a broiler for just a moment, it becomes firm and can hold the weight of your bites. Don't be afraid to be adventurous with bread: An olive loaf would go well with an Italian or Greek board, and a dark rye is a great pick for breakfast. For the best and freshest selection, visit the bakery early on the morning you are serving your board.

CRACKERS

One walk down the cracker aisle will give you no shortage of options. My advice for crackers is to stick to something simple; let the cheese, the meat and the dips be the stars of the board. Plain, artisan (I love something darker with a bit of substance) or rice are all good choices for crackers. Be wary of crackers sold in a bag instead of a sleeve, though;

there is nothing more disappointing than opening up a bag to find half the crackers broken!

ACCOMPANIMENTS

DIPS, SPREADS, MUSTARDS & PRESERVES

Everyone loves a good dip. Whether they're holding a chip, cracker or hunk of baguette, people love to schmear on a good spread. When selecting your dips and spreads—either from the recipes in this book or premade from your grocery store—think about how they work with the heroes of your board. If you're featuring rich cheeses and meats, skip the creamy dip and go with a mustard or jelly instead. If your board is heavy on vegetables, consider two different spreads with the same base, like a duo of hummus. Always provide separate serving utensils for every dip you put on a board. And remind your guests of the golden rule of no double dipping!

SWEET TASTES

A grazing board should always have some sort of sweet component. Creamy cheeses and fatty charcuteries weigh heavy on the palate, and without something to reset your taste buds, the nuances of the main events can be lost. Fruit is always a good choice (see page 16). If choosing fresh, I recommend grapes or berries. They're already bite-size and offer a burst of brightness in both flavor and color. Stone fruits and melons are also good choices. Besides being incredibly juicy, they don't tend to oxidize, so they keep looking good. Dried fruit is excellent to keep on hand for boards. I store an assortment in my crisper and often choose a few dried apricots or cherries to fill empty spaces on my boards. Other forms of sweet relief can come from honey (or better yet, honeycomb) or sweet preserves.

BRINE

Most boards need a cleansing briny element to bring out the best of the other components. You don't need to have one of each item per person, just enough variety for everyone to try something. Visit the olive bar at your grocer for a selection of olive varietals. And look for different pickled vegetables available. The traditional pickle—the cucumber—can be found in many different forms. Cornichons are always a safe bet, sweet pickles are great for kids and a mustard pickle pairs delightfully with cured beef or ham. I also like spicy green string beans, beets and onions. And don't forget the fruits. Pickled cranberries (see page 170) burst in your mouth and revive your taste buds.

MAKE IT A MEAL

For some boards, I make suggestions of dishes you could make and serve to round out the board with a bit more sustenance. The meal pairings are meant to complement and elevate the board into a full meal. For example, a minestrone soup is the perfect accompaniment to the Joys of Spring board (page 69), and what better to serve with Trio of Hummus (page 52) than grilled chicken kebabs?

NUTS

Every board can benefit from a selection of nuts. Whether you're offering one type or an assortment, you really can't go wrong. Unless it's game day and you're going for the theme of shells on the floor paired with beer, I recommend stepping outside the box of regular peanuts. Pecans, walnuts, pistachios and almonds are my four go-tos. Nuts are the last thing I add to a board before garnishing it, because they fill any empty holes. A great seasonal accompaniment for a Christmas board is a bowl of in-the-shell nuts with a few nutcrackers. Nuts can also be roasted with herbs like rosemary and served warm; candied or dipped in chocolate for a sweet relief; crushed and rolled into a creamy chèvre (see Baby, It's Cold Outside, page 83) or baked on Bries (see Dreaming of a White Christmas, page 102).

SPECIAL DIETS

Entertaining can sometimes be an exercise in culinary wizardry as you navigate different diets and allergies. One of the beautiful things about a board is that it can be tailored to suit nearly all dietary requirements. If the diet restriction is moderate, your guest can simply navigate the board themselves and avoid certain items. For more serious restrictions, here are some suggested gluten-free and vegan alternatives.

GLUTEN-FREE

Try the following substitutions for guests who follow a gluten-free diet.

• Rice-based crackers (rather than wheat-based crackers).

• Salami chips (rather than crostini): Lay thinly sliced pieces of salami on a baking sheet and bake at 400°F for about 8 minutes or until the chips are crisp.

• Parmesan chips (rather than crackers): Grate small piles of Parmesan, about 2" in diameter, onto a baking sheet and bake at 400°F for 8 minutes.

• Crunchy, round vegetables (rather than crostini or crackers): Using a mandoline, slice kohlrabi, beets or turnips about ⅛" thick. Serve fanned out, just like you would crackers.

VEGAN

When preparing a vegan board, substitute regular cheese with homemade options (see my quick recipe for a sensational cashew ricotta on page 171) or prepackaged dairy-free choices. For meat substitutes, think about the flavor and texture that meat adds to a board—something chewy, salty and a bit smoky—and replace with dehydrated vegetables like beets or carrots, pickled beans or smoked tofu. You can also try the Vegan Vibes board on page 58. ∎

Create

THE BIG PICTURE

One of my main reasons for writing this book was to show how anyone can create a beautiful board. As I was working through each board, I realized that my method has a pattern based on a handful of simple techniques. This section will give you the basics of those techniques, and then it's over to you and your imagination!

Start by working out the purpose of your board: Who's going to be eating from it? Why are people coming over? Are you celebrating something special? Having an idea of why you're gathering helps you curate the board accordingly. For example, if you're celebrating your sister's birthday, focus on her favorite flavors. For children, I always include a mild cheese, a simpler cracker or a vegetable that they will recognize.

Next is location: Where and when are you getting together? I love a good kitchen party as much as the next girl, but my ideal night is huddled around an outdoor fire as the red wine and a board are passed around.

GETTING STARTED

You'll see on the boards pages that I don't detail how and where to place the components exactly. That's because there is no right or wrong way, just your way! Of course, there are a few tried-and-tested techniques that can help you get started. Here are my top tips for putting together your board:

• *Break up like colors.* Nestle a colorful vegetable between a pale cheese and crackers. If you have two green vegetables, don't put them side by side.

• *Spread out large amounts of one ingredient.* If you're planning to serve 16 slices of meat, for example, put it on at *least* four different parts of the board.

• *Apply photography composition rules.* Generally speaking, odd numbers are more visually appealing than even. Also, create a path for the eye to follow. If you have a dominant color or ingredient, consider arranging it on the board so it loosely looks like a letter *S* when viewed from above (see the green grapes in Thanksgiving Feast, page 99).

• *Feel free to be abundant or minimalist or anywhere in between.* I'm partial to very full, overflowing boards. You may prefer a little more breathing space between the components. It's absolutely personal preference. You can always start out sparse and fill until you feel it looks best.

• *Don't forget about the edges.* A Mexican Fiesta (page 112) and Baby, It's Cold Outside (page 83) are examples of how styling around the board can enhance the board itself. Linens, fresh flowers and other elements can be used to elevate the theme of the board and add to its beauty overall.

PUTTING IT TOGETHER: STEP BY STEP

The more boards you make, the more you'll find your own way of working. There's usually a hero or star of the board—it may be a new cheese you discovered at the farmers market or a killer dip recipe you've been dying to try—and then everything else tends to follow from there. Putting a board together is more of an art than a science, but here's how I do it, step by step:

1 *Lay out all the components* (photo on p. 20). This helps you visualize where they'll all fit and ensures you don't forget anything. I often leave whole meats like hard salamis or whole blocks of cheese in their original packaging if the board isn't going to be eaten for a few hours. I won't remove the plastic wrap until just before I serve the board, but I'll know exactly where everything will be placed ahead of time.

2 *Start with the biggest items*, which usually means the blocks of cheese. Space the cheeses out and consider keeping them toward the edges of the board to make it easier for people to slice them. I separate similar colors and flavors and keep blue cheese slightly isolated from the other cheeses so as not to transfer its aromatic aggression to its neighbors. (See Hoppy Easter, page 91) Just before serving, I slice a few pieces from each type of cheese to encourage everyone to dive in.

Other big items are often whole salamis. Keep these at the outer edges of the board as much as possible to make them easier to access. Place them between the cheeses, but don't let them touch. You'll place sliced meats later (see step 5), unless you want to fan them out in a row (see Lunar New Year Feast, page 131), in which case place them on the board now.

3 *Add any bowls that will hold dips, preserves or other components.* If you're not serving the board immediately, use the empty bowls as placeholders and fill them later. This way, if you're nuzzling up ham slices or sliced veggies, they'll have something to support them. If you have a lot of small bowls on a board (see Crostini for a Crowd, page 47), write what's going in each bowl on little pieces of paper so you don't forget.

4 *Add grapes, if using.* These are a staple on most of my boards because they're a source of juicy brightness among creamy cheeses and salty, fatty meats; they're available year-round in a multitude of varieties and colors; and they can sit out for extended periods. Take the time to snip them into clusters of four to six grapes, then pile them up so your guests don't have to pick them off the vine.

5 *Arrange other mid-size components.* Now you have a choice. You can spread out slices of meat around the board, then add the fruits and vegetables and then the bread or crackers, arranging and rearranging as you go. Or you can work through the board, left to right, alternating all of the aforementioned components until the board is complete.

(Continues)

6 *Add the small, individual items* such as nuts, dried fruits or individual berries. Nuts and dried fruits are great to tuck into small holes or fill areas around the edges of the board. Fresh berries add pops of color.

7 *Add a garnish.* Flowers are a fabulous way to garnish a board, but they must be food-safe. Food-safe pansies, sunflowers and nasturtiums are all readily available and are colorful choices. Greenhouses are a great source of edible or food-safe blooms. Visit the herb and vegetable section and look for plants that have started to go to seed or have naturally occurring blossoms, such as lavender, thyme or chives. Or add a sprinkle of pea shoots or microgreens just before serving.

8 *Step back and admire your work of art.* Make any final tweaks and adjustments and add serving tools like tongs and cheese knives. If you're storing the board in the fridge, remember to pull it out 30 to 60 minutes before serving to let the cheese come to room temperature. ■

Step 8

THE BOARDS

Everyday

BOARDS

BRING OUT THE BAGELS

SERVES 6

If you're serving this as a breakfast or brunch board, serve it with coffee or fruit-infused sparkling water. If you're taking it on a picnic, a rosé or Pinot Gris will be your best choice.

A bagel board is a simple platter borne out of the need to provide a quick but satisfying breakfast for overnight guests. A traditional hot breakfast often means cooking to order, and not much can be prepared in advance. The bagel board is the perfect solution for mornings when you have people rising at different times—and let's be honest, mini bagels are adorable. If you can't find the small ones, cut larger bagels into halves or even quarters. I always include sweet and savory elements. And this board isn't just for breakfast; it also makes a great picnic lunch!

PREPARATION

Make the Pickled Shallots and serve in a small bowl. For a more pungent kick, prepare them the day before you plan to serve this board.

Prepare the fruit and vegetables: Cut the lemon into 8 wedges. Cut the tomatoes into just under 1/4" slices. Cut the cucumbers into thin coins. Using a mandoline or a very sharp knife, cut the onion into paper-thin slices.

Prepare the other components in the style that works best for you (see page 23 for tips) then arrange everything on and around your board. Top with optional garnishes. Set out a toaster for anyone who wants a warmed or toasted bagel. Come together and enjoy!

TIPS

If you don't like lox, try a nice deli ham like honey or Black Forest instead. If you need a gluten-free or low-carb alternative, substitute the bagels with gluten-free bread or rice cakes.

Pickled Shallots (page 168)

Black grapes, 2 cups
Assorted fresh berries (blueberries, raspberries, blackberries), 1 cup
Lemon, 1
Tomatoes, 2 medium
English cucumbers, 2 small
Red onion, about 1/2 medium

Lox, any type, 6 oz

Whipped cream cheese, vanilla or plain, 8 oz
Spreadable white or goat cheese (e.g., Boursin), 6 oz

Mini bagels, 18

Fresh dill, flat-leaf or curly parsley and mint, for garnish
Fresh edible flowers, for garnish
Fresh fig, for garnish

BREAKFAST CROSTINI

SERVES 4 (V)

This toast board is my version of a crostini board for mornings. Toast doesn't have to be boring—just look at all the different versions of avocado toast! I like to make this board on a Saturday morning that's jam-packed with activities. Living in a major city, we find our home is the "host hotel" for many friends and family who have kids playing in tournaments. Unfamiliar field locations or game times can make for hectic mornings, but this board will get everyone out the door on time with a nutrient-dense breakfast inside them. Everyone can create the combination that best suits their palate.

PREPARATION

Prepare the fruit and vegetables: Slice the bananas in half lengthwise and leave the cut sides down to prevent browning. Cut the grapefruit into wedges. Last minute: Slice the avocado.

Toast the bread.

Prepare the other components in the style that works best for you (see page 23 for tips) then arrange everything on and around your board. Top with optional garnish.

TIPS

Jam and honey would be great additions or easy substitutions for this board. Some of my favorite toast topping combos are peanut butter, banana and chia seed; cream cheese, strawberries and coconut; peanut butter, granola and sunflower seeds; and avocado, chia and a squeeze of grapefruit juice.

Serve gluten-free granola in a slightly bigger bowl with a side of milk or yogurt for a gluten-free option.

Strawberries, 10, stems attached

Bananas, 2 large

Grapefruit, 1

Avocado, 1 large

Whipped cream cheese, 8 oz

White sandwich bread, 3 slices

Brown sandwich bread, 4 slices

Granola, 1 cup

Peanut butter, smooth or crunchy,
    1 cup

Sunflower seeds, 3 Tbsp

Unsweetened coconut flakes, 3 Tbsp

Chia seeds, 3 Tbsp

Fresh thyme, for garnish

EGGS & SOLDIERS BRUNCH BOARD

SERVES 8 (V)

 It's brunch, so consider setting up a mimosa or Bloody Mary station.

If you don't have a lot of confidence in the kitchen or are intimidated by the thought of making a breakfast to order, this is your board. Anyone can make toast. Anyone can boil water. With those two skills, you can put together this bright and cheerful board in no time. It can be made and assembled almost entirely the night before and is easily scalable depending on the size of your crowd. All that's required the morning of is to make the toast and slice the avocado.

PREPARATION

Prepare the fruit and vegetables: Slice the grapefruit into wedges. Cut off the tough parts of the asparagus spears and blanch the spears in boiling water until just fork-tender, then remove immediately into an ice bath. Snip the grapes and tomatoes into small clusters. Last minute: Slice the avocado into wedges.

Cook the eggs: Bring a pot of water to a boil. Gently lower the eggs into the water. Boil the eggs for exactly 6 minutes. Immediately drain and run the eggs under cold water. Place the eggs on the board or in the fridge until you're ready to use them. (They'll stay runny if you keep them in the fridge for up to 2 days.)

Toast the bread and slice into thin strips.

Prepare the other components in the style that works best for you (see page 23 for tips) then arrange everything on and around your board. Nestle in the optional garnishes.

TIPS

Alternatively, offer two kinds of toast—a dark rye or whole wheat and a lighter white bread like brioche or sourdough. Place a small dish of specialty salt, such as truffle or smoked, next to the board for guests to sprinkle on their eggs. Guests with gluten allergies could dip ham-wrapped asparagus into the soft egg.

Green grapes, 3 cups
Strawberries, 8, stems attached
Cherries, 8
Grapefruit, 1 large
Asparagus, 16 spears
Cherry tomatoes on the vine, 12
Avocado, 1 large

Honey ham, 15 slices

Mild white cheddar, 8 oz
Whipped cream cheese, 8 oz

Eggs, 8, room temperature

White sandwich bread, 8 slices

Fresh edible flowers, for garnish
Gooseberries, for garnish
Small pear, for garnish

EUROPEAN BREAKFAST

SERVES 4

 A slow and quiet French-press coffee is the perfect accompaniment to this simple board.

North American breakfasts can be quite gluttonous—the grand slam farmers 4 eggs with pan-cakes and a side of sausage type of fare. In contrast, many European countries take a simpler approach to their morning meal. This board celebrates the European breakfast. It's simple enough to be scaled down for just you and a loved one on a Sunday morning, and it's interest-ing enough to serve to guests. There is minimal work involved here; you could boil and peel the eggs the night before, but when it takes only 6 minutes to boil the perfect egg (not too hard, not too soft), why not do it in the morning while everyone is wiping the sleep out of their eyes?

PREPARATION

Make the dukkah spice and set aside.

Bring a pot of water to a boil. Gently lower the eggs into the water. Boil the eggs for exactly 6 minutes. Immediately drain and run the eggs under cold water. Peel the eggs and roll them in the dukkah spice. (The eggs can be made the day before and stored in the fridge.) Slice them into halves or quarters.

Toast the bread, cut off the crusts and slice into triangles.

Prepare and serve the other components in the style that works best for you (see page 23 for tips) then arrange every-thing on and around your board. Top with optional garnish.

TIP

Dukkah, one of my favorite spice blends, is available online or in specialty grocers if you don't want to make your own.

Dukkah spice, 4 Tbsp (page 140)

Black and green grapes, 3 cups total

Salami, 8 oz

Brie, any type, 7 oz

Eggs, 4, room temperature

Rye sandwich bread, 4 slices
White sandwich bread, 4 slices

Raspberry balsamic preserve, 1/3 cup
Spiced apricot preserve, 1/3 cup
Sicilian green olives, 8

Chive flowers, for garnish
Pea shoots, for garnish

PLAYFUL PLAYDATE PLATTER

SERVES 4-8 KIDS   (V)

Make a big pitcher of fruit–infused water.

When it comes to boards for kids, I strive to hit three points: healthy-ish, portable and unexpected. This board was inspired by an afternoon playdate. As the kids played, the moms sipped bubbly and enjoyed a beautiful grown-up lunch. Instead of hotdogs or mac 'n' cheese, the kids were treated to mini croissants and peanut butter fluff dip. And while treats like M&M's were on the board, there was also a healthy balance of fresh fruits and proteins to choose from. Kids love edible containers, so I used waffle cups and cones so they could grab and go.

PREPARATION

Make the Peanut Butter Fluff Dip and serve in a small bowl.

Prepare the fruit: Toss the cantaloupe cubes with the grapes and raspberries and fill the waffle cups. Core the apples, then with the top of the apple flat against a mandoline, slice the apples into ⅛" slices. If not serving right away, cover the apple slices with water and squeeze the juice from half a lemon over top. Last minute: Cut the bananas into ½" coins just before serving.

Lay the waffle cones on the board or stand them up in a shallow jar for 2 different presentations. (I use ½-pint mason jar in the photo.) Toss the popcorn with the alphabet pretzels. Fill each waffle cone with the popcorn mixture and top with M&M's.

Arrange everything on and around your board (see page 23 for tips) and wait for the smiles!

TIPS

Most of the board serving sizes in this book are based on adults, but this one's for kids. This board shows 4 cones, but there's plenty of food to feed up to 8 kids if you add a cone for each child. Word of warning: for a kids board, make sure there's the same number of treats for each child!

If you're serving children with peanut allergies, omit the assorted nuts and make the Peanut Butter Fluff Dip with almond or cashew butter, for example, or a nut-free cookie spread.

Peanut Butter Fluff Dip (page 178)

Bananas, 2

Apples, 1 per person

Apricots, 1 per person

Cantaloupe, cubed, 1 cup

Grapes, any color, 1 cup

Raspberries, 1 cup

Mini croissants, at least 1 per person

Waffle cups, 1 per person

Waffle cones, 1 per person

Popcorn, popped, 4 cups

Alphabet pretzels, 1 cup

Yogurt-covered pretzels, 1½ cups

Assorted gummies, ⅓ cup

Assorted nuts, ⅓ cup

M&M's, 4 Tbsp

NO GROWN-UPS ALLOWED

Let me start by saying you do not need a whale-shaped board to make this cute platter. It certainly helps, but it's by no means necessary. I love this board for an impromptu Friday-night playdate that includes the grown-ups. The key assembly note on this board is putting food on sticks. This allows kids to pick up their own serving, minimizing the risk of a bunch of fingers touching everything. The cheese-stuffed tortellini and simple marinara are served cold like a deconstructed pasta salad. Keeping the flavors mild but varied is a great way to introduce kids to new foods.

PREPARATION

Make the Ranch Dip and serve in a small bowl.

Prepare the fruit and vegetables: To make watermelon sticks, place the watermelon cut side down on a cutting board. Cut slices about 1″ wide. Rotate the cutting board 90 degrees and cut slices perpendicular to the other slices, also about 1″ wide. Thread the blueberries onto 8 toothpicks. Cut the grape tomatoes in half and set aside.

Using a mandoline, slice the cucumbers and carrots into 1/8″ slices. Set aside about 16 cucumber slices for the tortellini skewers. Alternating carrots and cucumbers, thread the vegetables onto 8 toothpicks.

Make the tortellini skewers (this can be done the day before): Cook the tortellini as per package instructions, but reduce the cooking time by 1 minute. Do not overcook. Drain the pasta and rinse with cold water. Thread a tortellini onto a toothpick, followed by a cucumber slice, half a bocconcini ball, another tortellini and half a tomato. Continue this method, alternating tortellini, vegetables, and cheese and putting at least 2 tortellini on each skewer. You can pop any unused bits and pieces into bowls.

Add the marinara sauce to a small bowl and prepare the other components, making sure they are sized for small hands. Arrange everything on and around your board (see page 23 for tips).

Ranch Dip (page 143)

Watermelon, 1/2 medium
Cherries, 2 cups
Blueberries, 1 cup
Grape tomatoes, 16
Baby or small English cucumbers, 4
Carrots, 2 large

Turkey breast, 16 slices
Ham sausage, 1 ring, 10 oz

Bocconcini, 16 balls, halved
Mozzarella, 12 slices or 8 oz
Babybel cheese, 8

Soda crackers, 40
Goldfish crackers, 1 cup

Cheese tortellini, 1 package
Marinara sauce, 1 cup
Fresh edible flowers and pea shoots, for garnish

TIP

If you're worried about the sharp toothpicks provoking an emergency-room visit, you can stack the cucumber and carrot coins around the board and put the blueberries and tortellini in separate small bowls.

PICNIC IN THE PARK

SERVES 8

A warm weekend is the perfect excuse to pack a blanket, a bottle of bubbly and a board to enjoy in the great outdoors. The best part of this picnic board is that most of its components benefit from being made the night before. On the morning of your picnic, just pack them into your basket or cooler and off you go. The pressed sandwiches sit for 4 hours or overnight in your fridge, under the weight of a cast-iron pan or other heavy object, making them compact and portable and melding the flavors beautifully.

PREPARATION

Make the Whipped Chèvre Dip and serve in a small bowl.

Prepare the pressed sandwiches: Slice a square focaccia loaf in half lengthwise. Slice the mozzarella balls into ¼" slices and place on the bottom half of the bread. Next add the mortadella, followed by the basil. Drain the sun-dried tomatoes and layer them onto the basil. Place the top half of the bread on top. Wrap tightly in plastic wrap. Place the sandwich in the fridge and top with a heavy item such as a cast-iron pan or sheet pan with a heavy item on top. Press the sandwich for 4 hours or overnight. When ready, cut into 8 equal sandwiches, wrap in parchment and secure with twine.

Prepare the fruit and vegetables: Snip the grapes into small clusters. Cut off the tough parts of the asparagus spears and blanch the spears for 3 minutes, then remove immediately into an ice bath. Pat dry and divide into 8 equal portions. Wrap each bundle securely with a piece of prosciutto. These can be made up to 24 hours in advance.

Prepare the other components in the style that works best for you (see page 23 for tips) then arrange everything on and around your board. Top with optional garnish.

TIP

For a lighter or simpler meal, replace the sandwiches with a plain baguette.

Whipped Chèvre Dip (page 149)

Pressed sandwiches:
    Focaccia bread, large
    Fresh mozzarella log, 8 oz
    Mortadella, 12 thin slices
    Fresh basil leaves, 1 cup
    Sun-dried tomatoes, 7 fl. oz,
        drained if packed in oil

Green grapes, 2 cups

Cherries, 12

Asparagus, 40 very skinny spears,
    fewer if thicker

Cherry tomatoes, 8 small

Celery, 4 long stalks

Prosciutto, 8 thin slices

Toscano cheese soaked in Syrah, 8 oz

Rosemary and olive oil Asiago
    cheese, 6 oz

Root vegetable chips, 7 oz bag

Castelvetrano olives, 16

Currants, for garnish

BRUSCHETTA BOARD

SERVES 8 (V)

 Grilled steak and potatoes are a perfect main course after this bright starter.

 To match the acidity of the tomatoes, pair this with a Sauvignon Blanc or Fiano.

Bruschetta (pronounced brus-ketta) is an appetizer from Italy that consists of grilled bread rubbed with raw garlic and topped with olive oil and salt. Traditionally, bread that was going stale was roasted over coals and used to taste-test the latest batch of olive oil. Since being adopted in North America, bruschetta has gone through several variations, one of the most popular being toasted bread topped with tomatoes, basil, olive oil and salt. This board is at its best in late summer or early fall when tomatoes are in abundance and the varieties available make for the most beautiful color scheme.

PREPARATION

Prepare the vegetables: Set aside a few of the tomatoes to be placed whole on the board. Cut the larger tomatoes into wedges and set aside. Dice the smaller tomatoes into smaller pieces. Place them in a fine-mesh sieve over a bowl to let some of the juice drain out.

Cut off the tough parts of the asparagus spears and blanch the spears briefly. If the spears are very thin, serve them raw.

Slice the bocconcini into halves. Slice the fresh mozzarella into ¼" slices. Place the burrata whole into a shallow dish.

Make the dressing: In a small jar (about the size of a baby-food jar), mix the balsamic glaze and 7 Tbsp of the olive oil with the dried basil, oregano, salt and pepper. Place on the board with a small spoon.

Arrange the tomatoes, asparagus, fresh basil, olives and cheeses on the board. Drizzle the remaining 1 Tbsp oil over the tomatoes, asparagus and cheese (avoid the fresh basil to prevent it from getting soggy). Garnish with fresh greens. Finish the entire board with a sprinkling of salt and pepper.

Slice half the baguette into about 2" pieces, leaving the other half intact. Leave the knife next to the baguette so guests can help themselves to more, if they like.

TIPS

Smaller tomatoes are best for this board. Look for colorful packages of yellow, green and red varietals. A quick grape/cherry tomato cutting tip: Get two plastic lids of about the same size. Lay out a few tomatoes on one lid and place the other lid on top. With one hand applying gentle pressure to the top lid, use a very sharp knife and slowly cut through the tomatoes.

For a more traditional bruschetta, add some halved garlic cloves to the board to be rubbed on the bread before topping with tomatoes. For an unexpectedly delectable bite, serve the bruschetta board alongside a board of fresh strawberries and mint topped with a drizzle of olive oil and vinegar and a pinch of salt and pepper.

Assorted grape, cherry or on-the-vine tomatoes, 8 cups total

Asparagus, 24 thin spears

Fresh basil, 2 cups or 1 small plant

Bocconcini, 10 small balls

Fresh mozzarella, 1 large ball

Burrata, 1 large ball

Dressing:

    Dark balsamic glaze, ¼ cup

    Extra virgin olive oil, 8 Tbsp

    Dried basil, 1 Tbsp

    Dried oregano, 1 Tbsp

    Flaked sea salt

    Coarse ground black pepper

1 large crusty baguette (not pictured)

Kalamata olives, 8 to 10

Fresh greens (frisée, savory, etc.), for garnish

CROSTINI FOR A CROWD

SERVES 8

 With so many flavor combinations on a crostini board, a bottle of dry, sparkling rosé is the way to go.

For those spur-of-the-moment nights when the weather is just right and you want to host some friends al fresco at home, this is the board. Crostini *in Italian means "little toasts." A crostini board is a choose-your-own-adventure offering that brilliantly outsources to your guests the task of creating the perfect bite. While some combinations may be obvious, others not so much. I highly encourage you to set out a few different flavor combinations to encourage the culinarily shy to step out of their comfort zone.*

PREPARATION

Make the Whipped Feta, Tomato Bacon Jam and Pea Pesto. Serve in bowls and jars placed around the board.

Prepare the fruit and vegetables: Cut the plums into small wedges and remove the pits. Use a mandoline to slice the cantaloupe ⅛" thick. Place the frozen peas in a small dish and let them thaw at room temperature. Using a mandoline, slice 2 radishes ⅛" thick; leave the other radishes whole, greens attached, as an edible garnish for the board. Using a mandoline, slice the baby cucumbers lengthwise into long strips ⅛" thick.

Thinly slice the baguette and toast it.

Place the olives and hazelnuts in small dishes. Drizzle the honey overtop the nuts, allowing it to coat them.

Arrange all the components on and around your board (see page 23 for tips), including plenty of fresh herbs.

TIPS

For the base, firm crackers or chips work great too. Make sure the toppings are bite-size so they perch on the crostini. Other garnishes could be a simple fleur de sel, spiced nuts or a balsamic glaze. When selecting the spreads, go for contrasting colors and complementary flavors.

Whipped Feta (page 171)
Tomato Bacon Jam (page 158)
Pea Pesto (page 150)

Plums, 2 large
Cantaloupe, ¼
Frozen peas, 1 cup
Snow peas, 1 cup
Radishes, 6, greens attached
Baby cucumbers, 2

Pepper salami, 24 thin slices
Prosciutto, 16 thin slices

Baguette, 1 large

Kalamata olives, pitted and sliced,
    ⅓ cup
Hazelnuts, ½ cup
Liquid honey, 2 Tbsp
Fresh dill, flat-leaf parsley and mint,
    small handful of each

UNDER THE SEA

SERVES 4

 An ice-cold sparkling Prosecco balances this board perfectly.

Seafood and cheese are not the easiest to pair with each other. Once you step outside the world of lox and cream cheese, it can get a little challenging. There are, however, some surprisingly delicious matches that may not be as obvious. Blue cheese is a delightful complement to smoked shellfish (think mussels and oysters) and goes well perched on a succulent prawn with a dollop of homemade cocktail sauce. Keep the seafood refrigerated until just before it will be eaten and consider serving it on a frozen salt block.

PREPARATION

Make the Smoked Trout Dip, Seafood Cocktail Sauce and Quick Pickled Onions. Serve in jars.

Prepare the fruit and vegetables: Snip the grapes into clusters of 4 to 6. Cut the lemon into 8 small wedges.

Preheat the oven to 400°F. Pat the prawns dry. Lightly oil a baking sheet and arrange the prawns in a single layer. Bake for 6 to 8 minutes until they transform from grey to pink and opaque. Lox usually comes presliced, so gently separate each slice so it's easy for guests to select. Serve the prawns and lox on a salt block or on ice (see below and page 10). Serve the smoked mussels directly from the tin.

Prepare the other components in the style that works best for you (see page 23 for tips), then arrange everything on and around your board. Top with optional garnishes.

TIPS

Juicy fruits like berries and grapes are important for a seafood board. They cut through the richness and smokiness of the fish and give the palate a break between bites.

A salt block is a great investment. It can be used to serve food hot or cold and makes for an attractive serving vessel. Don't overseason anything you put on a salt block, as the block itself will flavor the food. If you don't have a salt block, consider serving the seafood directly on ice.

Smoked Trout Dip (page 153)
Seafood Cocktail Sauce (page 153)
Quick Pickled Onions (page 168)

Green grapes, 2 cups
Blackberries, 8
Lemon, 1

Wild Pacific prawns, 16
Smoked trout fillet, 8 oz
Lox, any type, 6 oz
Smoked mussels, 2 oz tin

Crumbled blue cheese, 4 oz

Soda crackers, 24

Crème fraîche, ½ cup
Cornichons, ½ cup

Fresh curly-leaf parsley, for garnish
Fresh dill, for garnish

FRUIT & CHEESE BOARD

SERVES 8   (V)

This is both one of the simplest and most impressive boards you can bring to a gathering. There really are no wrong answers to the question "what fruit should I add?" It's about offering a vivid variety. If the board will be sitting out for several hours, avoid fruits that tend to turn brown quickly, like apples and bananas. After you've selected your fruit, choose one to three cheeses, with at least one being dippable. I like a sweetened whipped cream cheese if some guests are on the younger side.

PREPARATION

Make the Sweet Cream Dip and serve in a bowl.

Prepare the fruit: Snip the grapes into clusters of 4 to 6. Skewer the blueberries on toothpicks. Pit and slice the peaches into small wedges. Slice the watermelon into small wedges.

Position the cheeses on the board and pile up all of the fruit around them (see page 23 for tips). Top with optional garnishes.

TIPS

This board also makes a beautiful addition to a brunch. You can prepare it ahead of time so your guests can enjoy something bright and fresh while you're frying bacon and poaching eggs.

For a large gathering at lunch, you could pair it with the Bright & Blooming (page 71) or Powered by Plants (page 55) board alongside a build-your-own sandwich bar.

Sweet Cream Dip (page 178)

Red and green grapes, 4 cups total

Blueberries, 2 cups

Blackberries, 16

Raspberries, 16

Yellow cherries, 14

Strawberries, 10 large, stems attached

Plums, 8 small

Apricots, 4

Peaches, 2

Watermelon, 1 mini

Dragon fruit, ½ large

Papaya, ½ large

Fontina cheese, 9 oz

Jarlsberg cheese, 9 oz

Currants, for garnish

Fresh mint, for garnish

Fresh edible flowers, for garnish

TRIO OF HUMMUS

SERVES 8   (V)

 Grill some chicken skewers to turn this board into a complete meal.

Hummus is such a rich, creamy spread that it's best served with a crisp, cold drink, such as a Sauvignon Blanc.

While my passion is creating thoughtfully inspired boards, my reality is that I don't always have the time to create the extravagant board of my dreams. This hummus board is the answer. It's the ultimate fancy-not-fancy board. Hummus is so versatile and so forgiving that once you nail down the basic formulas, the possibilities for expressing your creative cleverness are endless. A surprise vegetable on this board is the kohlrabi. It's a gnarly-looking member of the turnip family that, when peeled, makes for a mild but crisp dipper.

PREPARATION

Make the Beet Hummus, Golden Hummus and Green Hummus. Serve in bowls.

Prepare the fruit and vegetables: Cut the lemon into wedges. Cut the bottom stem off the endive and gently peel away the leaves.

Slice off the tops and bottoms of the bell peppers and use your fingers to pull out each core. Slice through one side of each pepper so you can unroll the pepper into a long flat piece, with the inside of the pepper facing up. Run your knife along the inside of the pepper to remove any of the stem or white flesh. Starting on the left side, with the tip of the knife on the top corner of the pepper, slice off a triangle. Pivot your knife to the right to make another triangle. Alternate this method along the entire pepper.

Remove the stems from the kohlrabi and peel off the coarse outer skin. Cut the tops and sides until you have a rectangular shape. Cut into 1/4" slices. Cut the bottom inch off the broccolini stems. Blanch the broccolini, then plunge it into an ice bath. Pat dry before placing on the board.

Cut each pita into 8 triangles.

Arrange the vegetables and pita triangles around the three bowls of hummus (see page 23 for tips), and top with optional garnishes.

TIPS

If you want to skip the homemade hummus, head to your local grocer or farmers market. (Just make sure to hide the empty containers!) If you're feeling chef-y, hummus is a great spread to experiment with. Swap edamame beans or black beans for the chickpeas. Try avocado, plain yogurt or peanut butter instead of tahini. And get creative with flavor boosters like dried or fresh herbs, unexpected spices like cumin or cinnamon or pops of brightness with lime or grapefruit.

Beet Hummus (page 146)
Golden Hummus (page 148)
Green Hummus (page 149)

Lemon, 1 small
Carrots, 8 small, greens attached
Belgian endive, 2 heads
Red bell pepper, 1
Yellow bell pepper, 1
Orange bell pepper, 1
Kohlrabi, 1
Broccolini, 1 small bunch

Pitas, 8 large

Pea shoots, for garnish
Fresh edible flowers, for garnish

POWERED BY PLANTS

SERVES 4 (V)

 Cabernet Sauvignon is an ideal match for the meaty, aromatic intensity of the walnuts, mushroom pâté and olives.

Sometimes I feel bad for vegetarians. How often do they attend a lovely event, politely indicating in advance their dietary restrictions, only to be served a plate of uninspired crudités with a bowl of pasta? I think we can do better! In contrast to the usual bright platter of predictable vegetables, here's a board that's a little heartier and darker—meaty without the meat. Because of the sustenance and texture the dips provide, I chose to add only two cheese varietals and kept them firm and semifirm. It's important to know that the majority of cheeses are not strictly vegetarian.

PREPARATION

Make the Mushroom Pâté and Muhammara Dip. Serve in bowls.

Preheat the oven to 400°F. Spread the broccoli onto a baking sheet and drizzle with 2 Tbsp olive oil. Roast on the upper-third rack of the oven for about 10 minutes or until the tips of the broccoli start to darken. Let cool and finish with the flaked salt.

Thinly slice the baguette, drizzle with a little olive oil, and toast it.

Prepare the other components in the style that works best for you (see page 23 for tips), and arrange everything on and around your board. Top with optional garnishes.

TIPS

This board is meant to have a darker, moodier feel. It would be perfect for a cool fall or winter evening. If you opt to use store-bought dips for this, be sure to check the labels for animal products.

Mushroom Pâté (page 163)
Muhammara Dip (page 139)

Black grapes, 1½ cups
Cherries, 8
Broccoli, bite-size pieces, 4 cups
Extra virgin olive oil
Flaked sea salt, 1 tsp

Vegetarian Oka cheese, 7 oz
Vegetarian Fontina cheese, 9 oz

Fig and pistachio rye crackers, 12
Baguette, ½

Assorted olives, pitted, 16
Walnuts, whole or halved, ⅓ cup
Fig preserve, ⅓ cup

Fresh flat-leaf parsley sprigs, for garnish
Fresh thyme, for garnish
Fresh bay leaves, for garnish

EAT YOUR VEGGIES

SERVES 4   (V)

Give the vegetarians in your life a break from pasta. Now is the time to try a quiche or tart.

A sparkling fruit cooler continues this bright and cheerful color scheme.

You'll find no carrots or celery on this beautiful vegetarian board. While both are perfectly acceptable additions to many boards, there are so many other attractive and delicious options. There is also no cheese on this board. It's meant to be a board you could place next to a traditional meat and cheese board or bring as a striking addition to a potluck. A good vegetable board has at least one killer dip—on this board you get two, and both are perfect complements to any crunchy raw vegetable.

PREPARATION

Make the Dukkah Spiced Yogurt Dip and Green Goddess Dip. Serve in bowls.

Prepare the fruit and vegetables: Skewer the berries on small toothpicks. Alternate different berries or keep similar berries together. Cut the romanesco into bite-size pieces. Blanch the string beans. Snip the cherry tomatoes into clusters of 2 to 4. Place the grape tomatoes in a small bowl. Cut the radishes in halves or quarters. Slice the cabbage into small wedges, as if you were slicing orange segments. Using a mandoline, slice the fennel into thin slices. Last minute: Using a mandoline, slice the raw beet into 1/4″ slices just before serving, or store the slices in lemon water to prevent oxidization.

Serve the marinated peppers and olives in bowls. Arrange all the components on and around your board (see page 23 for tips). Top with optional garnishes.

Dukkah Spiced Yogurt Dip (page 140)
Green Goddess Dip (page 140)

Assorted fresh berries (blueberries, blackberries and raspberries), 2 cups total

Romanesco broccoli, 2 cups
Green string beans, 16 to 20
Red cherry tomatoes on the vine, 10
Yellow or orange grape tomatoes, 10
Radishes, 6
Red cabbage, 1/2 small head
Golden beet, 1 medium
Fennel, 1/2 bulb, white part only

Water crackers, 24

Marinated red bell peppers, 1/3 cup
Mixed nuts, 1 cup

Fresh thyme, for garnish
Fresh edible flowers, for garnish
Baby's breath, for garnish

VEGAN VIBES

SERVES 8   (V)

As a content carnivore, I don't cook a lot of vegan food, or at least not on purpose. However, with a rise in plant-based diets, everyone should have a simple go-to vegan recipe or two. The cashew ricotta on this board is creamy and rich, and when dolloped with a sweet preserve or fresh herb, it rivals any cow's milk creamery. The cashews also don't require an overnight soak, so if you have an hour, you can make vegan cheese. When you take away charcuterie from a board, you take away some of the salty, smoky and toothsome elements. I brought those elements back with the addition of a firm smoked tofu, blistered tomatoes and dried dates.

PREPARATION

Make the Cashew Ricotta Cheese and serve alongside the tomatoes (see below).

Prepare the fruit and vegetables: Snip the grapes into clusters of 4 to 6.

Blanch the string beans, then plunge them into an ice bath. Pat dry before serving. Cook the potatoes, covered, in 2″ of simmering water for 10 minutes or until fork-tender. Drain, drizzle with 1 Tbsp of the olive oil and season with salt and pepper. Let cool.

Preheat the oven broiler. Line a baking sheet with parchment. Place the tomatoes on the sheet, still attached to the vine. Drizzle with 1 Tbsp of the olive oil and place on the highest rack of the oven for 10 minutes. Keep a close watch. Tomatoes will be done when they have split or burst and have a char on the skin. Set aside and let cool.

Using a spiralizer or peeler, create ribbons with both carrots. Cut the bottom core off of the bok choy and separate each leaf.

Slice the baguette into ½″ slices and place on a baking sheet. Drizzle with the remaining 2 Tbsp olive oil and place under the broiler for 2 to 3 minutes. Flip the bread and toast for an additional minute, keeping a close eye so the bread doesn't burn. Use immediately or store in an airtight container until needed.

Serve the components in the style that works best for you, remembering the olives, dates, walnuts and apricot preserve, and arrange everything on and around your board (see page 23 for tips). Top with optional garnishes.

TIPS

To add richness to this board, consider including some Mushroom Pâté (page 163). Always read labels carefully if you're serving a strict vegan. Animal-derived products such as gelatin can show up in unexpected places. The same applies to alcoholic drinks. Many beers are filtered with bone char, and wines can be refined using isinglass, which is a fish product. Always ask to be sure.

Cashew Ricotta Cheese (page 171)

Grapes, any color, 2 cups
Green string beans, 24
Baby potatoes, 16
Cherry tomatoes on the vine, 12
Purple carrots, 2 large
Baby bok choy, 2 small bunches

Seasoning:
Extra virgin olive oil, 4 Tbsp
Flaked sea salt, 1 tsp
Coarse ground black pepper, 1 tsp

Smoked firm tofu, 8 oz

Artisan rye crackers, 16
Baguette, ½

Manzanilla olives, 12
Dates, 8
Walnuts, ¼ cup
Apricot preserve, ⅓ cup

Baby eggplant, for garnish
Fresh dill, for garnish
Pea sprouts, for garnish

DATE NIGHT IN

SERVES 2

By the time date night rolls around, we're ready for a drink! I like to experiment with a new cocktail or pull out that special bottle of wine we've been saving.

My husband and I have been enjoying "date night in" for over 20 years now. Long before we were parents, we recognized the importance of carving out time just for us. As much as we love to try new restaurants and socialize with friends, we have an even greater affinity for PJs and the stillness of our own kitchen. This board is such a relaxing way to start an evening in. After our son is in bed, one person is on cocktail duty while the other starts assembling the board. We keep this very simple. Some of our best boards were created from leftover bits and bites discovered in the fridge, but it's also nice to add at least one slightly more special element. I don't know about you, but I've always thought burrata was the sexiest cheese.

PREPARATION

Place the balsamic reduction and olive oil into the bottom of a small dish. Put the burrata in the same dish on top of the oil and vinegar. Around the edges of the burrata, place a few cherry tomatoes and some of the bread to encourage dipping.

Prepare the other components in the style that works best for you (see page 23 for tips), then arrange them on and around your board. Top with optional garnish.

TIP

This is a very small board, but if you're using it as your dinner for date night, you could make it more robust by adding a third meat and cheese or increasing the quantities all round.

You could also add a small lasagna or pizza, something easy that needs minimal prep and cleanup.

Cherry tomatoes, 6

Prosciutto di Parma, 4 slices
Soppressata salami, 4 slices

Ash-rind Brie, 1 small
Burrata, 1 small ball

Crusty bread, 8 thin slices

Olives, any type, 2
Caper berries, 2
Balsamic vinegar reduction, 2 Tbsp
Extra virgin olive oil, 2 Tbsp

Microgreen sprouts, for garnish

SOMETHING SWEET

SERVES 4 (V)

 If you're ready to move to an after-dinner drink, now is the time to open that dessert wine. Late-harvest Gewürztraminer and Moscatos are also good choices.

The end of a meal does not have to signal the end of an evening. Often at our home, dinner is done but wine glasses are still full and the conversation is still flowing. A dessert board is a perfect way to keep the evening going. The European tradition of serving cheese at the end of a meal is slowly catching on in North America—try cheese with a creamy, sweet or nutty profile—but I always add a small chocolate element for those who are looking for a more traditional sweet finish to the meal. The best part about this dessert? It's quick and easy and requires no baking!

PREPARATION

Make the Quick & Simple Chocolate Pudding and Roasted Apricot Preserve. Serve in bowls.

Cut the Brie into 8 slices.

Serve the fruit and other components in the style that works best for you. (If you can't find dried orange slices, slice fresh oranges into very thin rounds.) Arrange everything on and around your board (see page 23 for tips). Garnish with fresh mint.

TIPS

Flavor combinations that work well for this dessert board are wafer cracker, chocolate pudding and raspberries; wafer cracker, Stilton and apricot preserve; and Brie on top of chocolate pretzel.

Dried fruit is sweeter and has a more intense flavor than fresh. Try adding dried figs, apricots or blueberries. If you have the fresh varietal, try pairing it with the dried one. While almost any nut will work on a dessert board, almonds, hazelnuts, pecans and pistachios are safe standbys.

Quick & Simple Chocolate Pudding
(page 176)
Roasted Apricot Preserve (page 179)

Green grapes, 2 cups
Raspberries, 8
Apricots, 2

Brie log, 4 oz
Fruit-based Stilton, 8 oz

Thin savory wafer crackers, 16

Pecans, whole, ¼ cup
Dried (or fresh) orange slices, 8
Chocolate-covered pretzels, 8
Chocolate wafer cookies, 4
Fruit jellies, 4
Fresh mint, for garnish

CHOCOLATE CHARCUTERIE DESSERT BOARD

SERVES 8 (V)

This dessert board is bold and slightly adventurous. The showstopper, the chocolate salami, is guaranteed to impress your guests, yet requires just a handful of ingredients and about 20 minutes to prepare. The honey mellows the loud and boisterous blue cheese, one of the best varietals for a dessert board, making it a perfect pairing for the leftover wine from dinner or the sherry just being poured. Bright fresh fruit offers a lighter end to the meal, and the thin wafer cookies provide a textural twist to the board.

PREPARATION

Make the Chocolate Salami and serve directly on your board.

Prepare the fruit: Cut the grapes into clusters of 4 to 6. Thread the blueberries onto toothpicks.

Break the chocolate bar into rustic smaller pieces.

Arrange all the components on and around your board in the style that works best for you (see page 23 for tips). Drizzle the honey over the blue cheese. Garnish with fresh mint.

TIPS

Blue cheese is not always a crowd pleaser. It's best to flank it with sweet elements that will balance its strong, creamy profile.

If you'd rather not take a chance on blue, here are 4 other options: Aged Gouda (if it's at least 40 weeks old, it will have a butterscotch nuttiness that pairs very well with crisp apple slices sprinkled with cinnamon and sugar), Comté (accessible and mild, it's the perfect accompaniment to a bowl of sweet roasted nuts), chèvre (this tangy mild goat cheese is surprisingly great with very dark chocolate) or Pecorino (its brown-butter tones make it the perfect finish to a meal when drizzled with wildflower honey).

Chocolate Salami (page 173)

Red grapes, 3 cups
Blueberries, 1 cup
Strawberries, 6, stems attached

Aged blue cheese, 8 oz
Triple-crème Brie, 8 oz
Liquid honey, 2 Tbsp

Vanilla wafer cookies, 16
Dark chocolate bar with nuts and
    raisins, 4 oz
Salted caramels, 8

Fresh mint, for garnish

Seasonal

B O A R D S

JOYS OF SPRING

SERVES 4

Spring is the perfect time of year to invite friends over for some al fresco entertaining. As we shed heavy sweaters, we also say goodbye to holiday flavors like pumpkin and peppermint and welcome fresh tastes and colors like sweet peas and snap peas. This board combines the tart creaminess of herbed chèvre with a rich pâté heavy enough to warm bellies as the still-crisp air rolls in during the early evenings. Truly baby (young) carrots plucked from the garden offer a contrasting crunch to the smoother elements on this platter, and some briny olives and young strawberries round out all the notes.

PREPARATION

Prepare the fruit and vegetables: Baby carrots from the garden (not the bagged ones at the grocery store) will not need peeling; just give them a good washing to get the dirt off.

The pâté should be served at room temperature, so take it out of the fridge 30 minutes before serving.

Prepare the other components in the style way works best for you (see page 23 for tips), then arrange everything on and around your board.

TIPS

If rabbit pâté is too adventurous for you or your guests, you can stick with a traditional pâté or substitute with a thick-cut, toothsome herbed salami. A vegetarian alternative is the Mushroom Pâté (page 163) or a store-bought dip such as an Asiago and artichoke spread.

For larger groups, add more spring proteins like honey ham and lamb prosciutto or young cheeses like fresh mozzarella and Gouda, plus asparagus, fennel and apricots.

Strawberries, 4, stems attached
Snap peas, 12
Baby carrots, 8, greens attached

Herbed rabbit pâté, 8 oz

Herbed chèvre, 4 oz

Baguette, 1 small

Picholine olives, 12
Walnut pieces, 2 Tbsp

BRIGHT & BLOOMING

SERVES 4 (V)

 Add minestrone soup or an asparagus tart to round out this spring selection.

 Celebrate spring with bubbles and serve white wine spritzers or sparkling mimosas.

Spring offers plenty of reasons to entertain with bridal showers, graduations and garden parties. With the daffodils in full bloom and summer just around the corner, it's time to lighten everything up. This vegetarian board is bursting with bright color and makes the ideal centerpiece for a spring celebration. The farmers market is your best place to find all of the components for this board, as you can take advantage of the natural state of the vegetables that the farmers bring in, and a bright head of cabbage makes the perfect vessel for an herbed yogurt dip.

PREPARATION

Make the Herbed Yogurt Dip. Set aside.

Prepare the vegetables: Cut the carrots and cucumbers lengthwise into quarters, leaving 2" to 3" of green tops on the carrots. Remove a few outer stalks from the celery and use only the inside stalks. Cut the larger ones from top to bottom into thinner pieces, leaving the leaves attached.

To make the cabbage dip bowl, peel back a few of the outer layers of the cabbage. Slice about ½" off the bottom so it sits flat. Cut a small circle out of the top of the cabbage and use a spoon to scrape and shape the hole until it's big enough to hold about 1 cup of dip. Fill with Herbed Yogurt Dip.

Place the cheese in bowls and arrange all the components on and around your board (see page 23 for tips). Top with optional garnishes.

TIPS

Break up the whites and greens by alternating colors around the board and using brightly colored dishes. To make it a little heartier, add a basket of buns and butter with a small board of sliced ham.

Edible flowers are at their best in the spring as everything starts to blossom.

Herbed Yogurt Dip (Page 141)

Carrots, 8, greens attached
Baby cucumbers, 4
Cherry tomatoes, 2 cups
Snap peas, 2 cups
Cauliflower florets, 2 cups
Celery, 1 bunch
Cabbage, 1 small head

Burrata, 8 oz (or 1 large ball)
Bocconcini, 12 medium balls

Breadsticks, 1 package (or 25)

Baby kale or romaine leaves, for garnish
Fresh edible pansy flowers, for garnish

SAY HELLO TO SUNSHINE

SERVES 4

Fire up the grill! Kebabs are a simple, portable way to turn this board into a meal.

 The unmistakable light pink rosé is a classic summer drink.

Summer is probably the best season to make a beautiful board. Produce is at its peak, making everything vibrant not only on the outside, but on the inside too. There's nothing like the burst of freshness that comes from biting into a strawberry when it's at its peak. This summer board contains all that represents summer bounty: flowers, easy cheeses and meats, and bright vegetables. The corn is just barely steamed to maintain its crunch. And crisp in-season string beans make the perfect dippers for a creamy whipped feta.

PREPARATION

Make the Whipped Feta and serve in a small bowl.

Prepare the vegetables: Place about 2″ of water in a deep, heavy-bottomed pan and bring to a boil over high heat. Cut the cobs of corn into 2″ pieces, and steam for 5 to 7 minutes. Remove immediately. Taste a raw string bean; if you find it too bitter, steam the beans for a couple of minutes to mellow them out.

Prepare the other components in the style that works best for you (see page 23 for tips), then arrange everything on and around your board. Top with optional garnishes.

TIPS

Farmers markets are the best inspiration for summer boards. Each growing region has its own specialities, so don't be afraid to try a new varietal of your regular standby vegetable or fruit. Shop with the objective of finding one red, yellow, orange and green element for your board.

I like to use Grand Cru Surchoix for the raw cow's milk cheese on this board. If you or your guests need to avoid raw cheese for health reasons, Gruyère is a good substitute.

Whipped Feta (page 171)

Strawberries, 8, stems attached
Plums, 4

Green and yellow string beans, 16
Carrots, 8
Corn on the cob, 2 ears

Summer sausage, 7 oz
Whiskey salami, 6 oz
Prosciutto, 5 oz

Pesto Gouda, 6 oz
Raw cow's milk cheese or Gruyère, 6 oz
Chèvre, 4 oz

Small round wheat crackers, 25

Pickled orange baby bell peppers, 4

Baby kale, for garnish
Fresh edible flowers, for garnish

SUMMER VIBES

SERVES 4

 Add some pressed sandwiches and take this board to the beach for the day.

 A spiked strawberry-lemonade spritzer will keep you cool in the heat.

Summer is the perfect time to try fruits and vegetables from your local farmers market that you may not find at your grocery store. The plums on this board are called pluots—a hybrid of a plum and an apricot. You could offer regular plums, or any seasonal fruit, but I love adding something that has a familiar feel yet an unexpected twist. The fresh produce is the hero of this board, so there's only one cheese and meat, although each is robust with flavor and of high quality.

PREPARATION

Prepare the vegetables: If you prefer string beans with a little less crunch, blanch them prior to serving (see page 17). To add a little wow factor to the board, slice open a couple of the snap pea shells to reveal all the peas inside.

Prepare the other components in the style that works best for you (see page 23 for tips) then arrange everything on and around your board. Top with optional garnishes.

TIPS

This light board makes a perfect starter to a summer cookout, so when you're selecting items at the farmers market, grab some great grilling vegetables to add to the board like eggplant or asparagus, or even stone fruits like peaches and nectarines. You'll also find a great selection of edible blooms in summertime that add interest and pops of color like squash blossoms and nasturtiums, and herb blossoms like lavender and basil, or fruit blossoms like cherry or peach.

This board would also be great for a picnic. The components are all quite sturdy and pack well. Add a blanket and some bubbly and you're set for an afternoon in the park.

Pluots, 4

Snap peas, 12

Heirloom white box radishes, 8

Heirloom tomatoes, 8 small

Italian dry salami, 8 oz

Triple-crème truffle Brie, 7 oz

Mini fig and olive crisps, 16

Assorted pickled peppers and caper berries, 1/3 cup

Fresh edible nasturtiums and zucchini blossoms, for garnish

VEGETABLE HARVEST

SERVES 4   (V)

Try a butternut squash ravioli with sage butter and a salad with some of the same vegetables as the board.

The harvest season brings not only a change of color to the leaves but also a change in crops. Pattypan squash and candy cane beets are as fun to say as they are to dip into the roasted butternut squash hummus on this board. I kept the board vegetarian, since the fall crops are the star of the season. At this time of year, don't miss picking up some coronation grapes. These late-season gems are super-concentrated with a burst of sweet juice and a tart finish.

PREPARATION

Make the Butternut Squash Hummus and serve in a bowl.

Prepare the fruit and vegetables: Snip the grapes into clusters of 4 to 6. Cut the pattypan squash into quarters. Leaving the tops on the yellow zucchini, slice them lengthwise into quarters. Remove the stem and fronds from the fennel and cut the bulbs into small wedges. Peel the beet and, using a mandoline, finely slice it.

Prepare the other components in the style that works best for you (see page 23 for tips), then arrange them on and around your board. Top with optional garnishes.

TIPS

Combine late-fall produce like apples, pears, steamed parsnips and cauliflower on your board, and garnish with leaves, twigs and ornamental gourds for a festive tablescape. Wine country is in full swing for harvest season, so this is a great opportunity to introduce your guests to a small, obscure winery.

Butternut Squash Hummus
(page 148)

Coronation grapes, 3 cups
Pattypan squash, 10 small
Baby yellow zucchini, 4 small
Fennel, 2 bulbs
Candy cane beet, 1

Wensleydale apricot cheese, 7 oz
Shropshire blue cheese, 5 oz
Za'atar-infused chèvre, 5 oz

White soda crackers, 24
Pumpkin seeds (pepitas), 1/3 cup

Decorative gourds, for garnish
Gooseberries, for garnish

FALL FEAST

SERVES 8

A hard-cider sangria
complements the harvest
theme.

Fall is one of my favorite times of year to entertain. Whether it's for football, family, friends or just falling leaves, I love to celebrate the crisp-air nights and the opportunity to gather around outside with blankets and a warm fire. The color and flavor of this board are inspired by the bounty of the fall harvest. A fennel-laced salami and garlic-chive Cheddar Gouda blend are just some of the many fall elements that make up this feast.

PREPARATION

Make the Quick Carrot Jam and serve in a small bowl.

Prepare the fruit and vegetables: Snip the grapes into clusters of 4 to 6. Slice the cucumber lengthwise into quarters.

Prepare the other components in the style that works best for you (see page 23 for tips), then arrange everything on and around your board. Nestle in the optional garnishes.

TIPS

This board makes a perfect centerpiece to a longtable harvest dinner. By laying down butcher paper, you can recreate a narrower version of this board that runs the length of your table. Break up the components with ornamental squash and mini pumpkins.

Honeycomb adds a bit of wow factor to boards, and is available at most farmers markets and specialty food stores. It tends to run a bit, so you may want to place it on its own little board or even in a small dish. If you can't find honeycomb, serve regular honey in a small bowl on the board.

Quick Carrot Jam (page 160)

Coronation grapes, 3 cups
Snap peas, 12
Pickling or baby cucumber, 1 medium

Fennel salami, 16 slices
Bresaola, 16 slices

Chèvre, 5 oz
Smoked Cheddar, about 4 oz
Garlic and chive Cheddar-Gouda
    blend, 3 oz

Hearty fruit and nut crackers, 24

Honeycomb, 2″ × 2″ (see tips)
Dried apple slices, 16
Assorted olives, 16

Pear, 1 miniature, for garnish
Fresh fig, 1 small, for garnish

WINTER FONDUE

SERVES 8

 An ice-cold Riesling cuts through the richness of all the cheese.

A cold winter's night calls for a board that warms the soul. A fondue board answers that call perfectly. Cubed bread, a sausage ring and lots of ooey-gooey melted Gruyère are the stuff winter nights are made of. I remember the first time my mom made fondue back in the 80s. Couples showed up with their extra pots and skewers, and everyone had such fun dipping and dunking—it was my original cheese-board inspiration! Vibrant purple cabbage and crisp green string beans are some updated dipping vegetables.

PREPARATION

Make the Pickled Cranberries. Serve skewered onto wooden toothpicks.

Prepare the other fruit and vegetables: Snip the grapes into clusters of 4 to 6. Cut the broccoli into bite-size pieces and blanch for about 2 minutes. If the string beans are fresh and young, serve them raw; otherwise, blanch them with the broccoli. Slice the cabbage into small wedges.

Slice the sausage into bite-size pieces.

Slice the entire baguette into bite-size cubes.

When you're ready to serve, melt all the cheese in a small pot over low heat, and avoid stirring. When the cheese is fully melted, pour it into a fondue pot and light the flame or tealight. Retain any excess cheese on the stove off the heat and repeat the process to replenish as the fondue pot depletes.

Arrange all the other components around the fondue pot for easy dipping.

TIP

The 80s are over and fondue is much more than Gruyère. If the mix of cheeses suggested for this board doesn't appeal, try a goat cheese with buttermilk and chives; Stilton with crème fraîche and tarragon; Emmental with shallots and crab; or smoked mozzarella and cayenne pepper.

Pickled Cranberries (page 170)

Black grapes, 3 cups
Broccoli florets, 2 cups
Green string beans, 24
Purple cabbage, ½ medium head

Turkey sausage ring, 13 oz or 1 ring

Fondue cheese blend, 20 oz (see note
    on page 123)
Emmental cheese, 5 oz
Shropshire blue cheese, 3 oz

Baguette, 1 large

Fresh thyme, for garnish

BABY, IT'S COLD OUTSIDE

SERVES 4

 The beauty of an olive and cheese board is that most red wines will pair well with it. If you're considering a cocktail to start the evening, a gin-based one will pair best with the olives.

There's something particularly appealing to me about entertaining when it's cold out—greeting guests shaking off snowflake-dusted hats and sipping a big, bold glass of cabernet while enjoying the aroma of hearty goodness simmering on the stove. This is a starter board that kicks off an evening with a hearty meal to follow. The goat cheese is dressed up with a sweater of crushed nuts and dried cherries. The Wensleydale cheese is infused with cranberries to mark either the start of the holidays or their conclusion.

PREPARATION

Prepare a coating for the chèvre: Scoop ¼ cup of the nuts and dried cherries into a small resealable plastic bag. Using a heavy-bottomed glass, crush them and pour them onto a shallow plate. Roll the honey chèvre into the crushed nuts, gently pressing the nuts so they stick to the cheese.

Last minute: Preheat the oven to 350°F. Place the remaining nuts and the rosemary sprig on a baking sheet and warm in the oven for about 10 minutes. Serve warm in a bowl on the board.

Serve the other components in the style that works best for you (see page 23 for tips), then arrange everything on and around your board.

TIPS

The hero on this board is really the olive and cheese combination. It can easily be scaled up with the addition of more olive and cheese varietals (it can also be scaled down). To set a winter scene, wrap a clean white flour-sack towel or piece of cheesecloth under your board and scatter evergreen branches from the yard or snow-capped pinecones from a craft store around it.

Herbed salami, 12 slices
Schinkenspeck, 12 slices

Honey chevre, 5 oz
Wensleydale cranberry cheese, 5 oz

Breadsticks, 16

Assorted nuts with dried cherries,
   2 cups
Fresh rosemary, 1 sprig

Spiced Sicilian green olives, pitted, 8
Castelvetrano olives, 8
Assorted red olives, 8
Caper berries, 4
Dried apricots, 4

Holiday &
Special Occasion

— BOARDS —

VALENTINE'S NIGHT IN

SERVES 2

 That bottle you've been saving for a special occasion.

There are nights my husband and I love to go out for dinner, but Valentine's Day isn't one of them. It falls on a weekday most years, which means a long workday is likely followed by a soccer game, piano practice or homework session. The thought of trying to squeeze in a big romantic dinner is usually too much for us. Instead, we choose to stay home and keep things simple. After the night has wound down, this board of high-quality Italian meats and creamy cheeses is our dinner, along with a side dish called a glass of fermented grapes. The best part is, dessert is included.

PREPARATION

Prepare the fruit: Snip the grapes into clusters of 3 to 5. Leave the berries whole.

Slice the baguette and serve fresh or lightly toasted.

Break the dark chocolate into random bite-size pieces for a rustic look.

Serve the other components in the style that works best for you (see page 23 for tips), then arrange everything on and around your board. Add microgreens and an optional red rose.

TIPS

Personalize this board by choosing meats, cheeses and accompaniments that reflect your and your partner's heritage.

Valentine's Day is a great excuse to sample more expensive cheeses, as you need just a small amount for 2 people. For this board, I selected an ash-coated artisanal blend of goat and cow's milk cheeses.

Black grapes, 1 cup
Blackberries, 4
Strawberries, 2, stems attached

Cacciatore, 8″ link
Prosciutto di Norcia, 6 slices

Baby Bries, 2
Artisanal mixed-blend cheese, 2 oz
    (see tips)

Baguette, ¼

Dark chocolate bar, 2 oz
Honeycomb, 2″ × 2″ (see tips on
    page 79)
Fig and onion jam, ¼ cup
Assorted olives, 6

Microgreens, for garnish

AND THE AWARD GOES TO

SERVES 8

 You already have the popcorn and chips, so award yourself the rest of the night off and order in.

 It doesn't have to be fancy, but bubbly is always the perfect pairing for an awards party.

For most people, celebrating the glitz and glam of the awards season means curling up on the sofa at home in their PJs with a bowl of popcorn. But it's also a great excuse to have some friends over and cast your own ballots for best picture. This board spills over a little thanks to two snack staples—chips and popcorn—that get dressed up for the party with edible gold leaf. A cheese and a salami are wine-soaked—just as some stars will be that night—and the board snacks are bundled and skewered, making for the perfect fancy finger food, whatever you're wearing.

PREPARATION

Make the Chocolate-Dipped Golden Potato Chips and Golden Bacon Popcorn. Serve in bowls alongside the board.

Make the star tortilla chips: Preheat the oven to 400°F. Using a star-shaped cookie cutter, cut star shapes out of the corn tortillas. Place in a single layer on a baking sheet and lightly brush both sides with the olive oil. Sprinkle one side with sea salt and place in the oven until crisp, about 10 minutes.

Cut off the tough parts of the asparagus spears and blanch the spears to serve slightly tender (very thin asparagus stems are fine to serve raw). Wrap a slice of wine salami snugly around a bundle of 2 to 4 spears, depending on the thickness of the asparagus. Repeat with the remaining salami and asparagus.

Cut the feta into 8 equal cubes. Skewer 1 olive and 1 piece of cheese onto 8 toothpicks.

Serve the other components in the style that works best for you (see page 23 for tips), then arrange everything on and around your board. Garnish with pea shoots.

TIPS

Everything for this board can be made ahead on the day of the awards show—a perfect red-carpet preview-show activity! I like to make about 3 to 4 chocolate-covered potato chips per guest and then mix regular chips into the bowl. The edible gold can be bought at most specialty kitchen stores or online.

Chocolate-Dipped Golden Potato Chips (page 176)
Golden Bacon Popcorn (page 174)
Star tortilla chips:
Corn tortillas (10″), 8
Extra virgin olive oil, 2 Tbsp
Flaked sea salt, 2 Tbsp

Green grapes, 2 cups
Asparagus, 24 thin spears

Bresaola, 16 thin slices
Wine salami, 8 medium slices

Toscano cheese soaked in Syrah, 9 oz
Italian truffle cheese, 9 oz
Feta, 2 oz

Castelvetrano and cerignola olives, 4 of each

Pea shoots, for garnish

HOPPY EASTER

SERVES 8

Easter traditions vary greatly around the world. From telling tales of the mythical bunny hiding chocolate eggs to recognizing a both somber and joyous occasion within the Christian faith, everyone marks Easter in their own way. The common thread for this holiday is bringing people together in a celebration around food. This board is the perfect bridge between your "breakfast" of chocolate eggs and the big feast later that evening. For this board, I started with proteins reminiscent of a traditional Easter dinner—lamb, ham and a duck pâté—then added complementary herbs and other accompaniments.

PREPARATION

Make the Vertical Deviled Eggs. Serve in egg cups or place directly on your board.

Prepare the fruit and vegetables: Snip the grapes into clusters of 4 to 5. Cut off the tough parts of the asparagus spears and blanch to serve slightly tender (very thin asparagus stems are fine to serve raw). Cut the cucumbers and carrots lengthwise into quarters, leaving 2" to 3" of green tops on the carrots. Cut the radishes into halves or quarters.

Place the burrata whole into a shallow dish.

Serve the other components in the style that works best for you (see page 23 for tips), then arrange everything on and around your board, with the challah to the side for easy slicing. Top with optional garnishes.

TIPS

If you feel there's too much meat in one pile, create several smaller piles or replenish as people eat. You can wrap a piece of prosciutto or ham around a couple spears of asparagus to break up the green and give your guests a flavor combination idea. The fresh mozzarella is mild and pairs well with most herbs. For a bolder taste, use a stronger fresh herb like chives, thyme or dill instead of parsley.

Younger guests will enjoy the sweet braided bread topped with a slice of creamy Havarti and wildflower honey ham. And they'll especially love it if you place egg cups around the board filled with some of the morning's treats!

Vertical Deviled Eggs (page 166)

Moscato (or green) grapes, 2 cups
Asparagus, 10 spears
Snap peas, 10
Baby cucumbers, 8
Carrots, 8, greens attached
Radishes, 8

Lamb prosciutto, 16 thin slices
Wildflower honey ham, 16 thin slices
Orange duck pâté, ½" slice

Burrata, 1 medium ball
Havarti cheese, 1 lb
Buttermilk blue cheese, 7 oz

Challah (braided bread), 1 large loaf
Fruit and nut crackers, 32

Grainy mustard, ¼ cup

Fresh chives, for garnish
Fresh edible pansies, for garnish

PASSOVER BOARD

SERVES 8

Follow the Seder plate with a festive meal of favorites, such as chicken soup and gefilte fish.

The traditional drink to serve alongside a Seder plate is 4 cups of red wine.

Passover is a meaningful occasion in mid-spring for which to prepare a bountiful board. It's celebrated by people of the Jewish faith to commemorate a time when, according to the Hebrew bible, God directed Moses to free the Israelites from slavery in Egypt. Once the sun sets on the first day of Passover, Jews conduct the Seder the traditional feast for Passover. Matzah replaces any sort of leavened bread at this time. Make certain to inquire if any of your guests are keeping kosher so you can create a modern interpretation of a Seder plate while respecting the tradition and its associated requirements.

PREPARATION

Make the Sweet & Smoky Deviled Eggs.

Prepare the vegetables: If the celery stalks are wide, run a knife from top to bottom to split them in 2 without removing the leaves. Leave the tomatoes whole.

Serve the other components in the style that works best for you (see page 23 for tips), then arrange them around the different salmon on the board. Top with optional garnishes. Finish the board with a light sprinkling of flaked sea salt on the eggs, celery and tomatoes.

TIPS

If you're serving a kosher board, every step of the process (from purchasing and storing to preparing and serving the food) must be kept kosher. Consult online resources, reach out to a local synagogue or ask one of your guests for guidelines.

Sweet & Smoky Deviled Eggs
(page 166)

Assorted grape, cherry or on-the-vine
tomatoes, 2 cups
Celery, 10 center stalks, leaves
attached on some

Sockeye salmon lox, 4 oz
Wild hot-smoked sockeye salmon,
4 oz
Peppercorn-crusted smoked salmon,
4 oz

Cream cheese, ⅓ cup

Matzah crackers, 16

Heirloom tomatoes, 2 to 4, for garnish
Fresh flat-leaf parsley, for garnish
Fresh dill, for garnish
Flaked sea salt, 1 Tbsp

GAME-DAY SNACK STADIUM

SERVES 8

It has to be ice-cold
beer in a frosty glass.

Are you ready for some football? Or baseball? Or even water polo? My house is a sports house. No matter what time of year, there is some kind of sporting event on our television. I have no doubt that the very first board I ever created was because we were having people over for a match of some kind. This particular board is all about simple, fun snacks. The layout is meant to represent a stadium surrounded by fans, and you can get as creative as your imagination allows! Just place one smaller board in the center of one larger board and start lining up the cracker-and-cheese fans.

PREPARATION

Make the Wedge Salad Dip and Buffalo Chicken Dip and set aside.

Prepare the vegetables: Slice each carrot lengthwise, leaving the top 1″ of greens attached. Slice the celery stalks lengthwise, keeping their leafy greens intact.

Slice the ham sausage into ½″ rounds. If using regular pepperoni sticks instead of mini ones, cut them into 3″ to 4″ pieces.

Slice the cheese into approximately 2″ × 3″ rectangles.

To assemble, place a smaller rectangular board in the center of a large rectangular board to create the illusion of a playing field surrounded by fans. Symmetry looks great on this board, so place the dips on top and alternate meat, cheese and crackers around the outside. Fill the "end zones" with loose potato chips, and add bowls at the stadium corners for pickles and vegetables.

TIPS

When your favorite fans arrive, have this board ready to greet them. At halftime, bring out the traditional game-day hot foods. This also makes a great kid-friendly board if you use a mild pepperoni.

Wedge Salad Dip (page 141)
Buffalo Chicken Dip (page 143)

Carrots, 8, greens attached
Celery, 8 center stalks, leaves
    attached

Ham sausage, 12 oz
Mini pepperoni sticks, 20

Pepper Jack cheese, 8 oz

Cheesy crackers, 1 box
Potato chips, 1 family-size bag of your
    favorite flavor
Assorted nuts and pretzels, 2 cups

Sweet pickles, 2 cups
Sweet pickled onions, 16

HAPPY HALLOWEEN

A candy-apple martini
works with the theme.

Halloween has reached a whole new level. When I was a kid, we carved one family pumpkin and used a pillowcase as a candy bag, and the holiday lasted two hours. Fast-forward to today, when Halloween is a month-long celebration! Regrettably, most of the food leans toward the gruesome side. And because peeled-grape eyeballs and pumpkins vomiting French onion dip are not my thing, the spookiest item you'll find here is chèvre shaped into a bone. But I love the idea of a dark board. Black grapes, espresso-crusted cheese and big Kalamata olives are all on theme and make a great contribution to a Halloween table.

PREPARATION

Snip the grapes into clusters of 4 to 6. Skewer the olives onto toothpicks, 2 per toothpick.

Remove the chèvre from its packaging and place on a cutting board. Cover with a large piece of plastic wrap and begin to shape it into the form of a bone. This will take some massaging and squishing and will be easier if the cheese is at room temperature. Smooth out any ridges or bumps with a small spatula or butter knife.

Prepare the other components in the style that works best for you (see page 23 for tips), then arrange everything on and around your board.

TIPS

Halloween is a great time to go for a dark board. I look for black-rind, espresso-crusted or ash-laced cheeses to complement the holiday theme. And it doesn't have to be gross: pipe plain yogurt over hummus in the form of a spider web, or add blackened chicken wings, black bean dip or anything pumpkin.

Black grapes, 2 cups
Blackberries, 8

Honey ham, 16 slices
Saucisson sec (salami), 2 links

Chèvre log, 11 oz, room temperature
Black-rind, beer-infused cheese, 8 oz
Espresso-crusted cheese, 6 oz

Pumpkin seed crisps, 16

Black olives, 8
Spicy pickled mushrooms

THANKSGIVING FEAST

SERVES 8

Offer a Pinot Noir with bright notes of cherry and cranberry or a buttery Chardonnay for the white wine–lovers.

Thanksgiving is the perfect occasion for a board whether you are the host or a guest. Some years we celebrate more of a casual Friendsgiving, coming together for a potluck-style night of sips and bites. For these times, I create this Thanksgiving board. It's a colorful collection of all that is Thanksgiving dinner: baby buns, sliced turkey, Brussels sprouts and the show-stopper, a creamy mashed potato dip.

PREPARATION

Make the Bourbon Pumpkin Butter, Mashed Potato Dip and Pickled Cranberries. Serve in bowls on the board.

Prepare the fruit and vegetables: Snip the grapes into clusters of 4 to 6. Steam the Brussels sprouts until fork-tender (7 to 9 minutes), pop them in an ice bath to stop them cooking, then cut them in half. Cut 4 slices of the speck into 4 equal pieces (keep the rest for arranging across the board). Thread one half of a Brussels sprout on a toothpick, followed by a piece of speck, then the bottom half of the sprout and finally another piece of speck. Repeat with all the sprouts.

Steam the string beans (you can do them with the Brussels sprouts—they will take less time, so add them when the sprouts have been steaming for about 3 minutes), then pop them in an ice bath. Cut the radicchio into small wedges. Trim the radish tops, leaving just under 1" of green stem.

Serve the other components in the style that works best for you (see page 23 for tips), then arrange everything piled up on the board for an overflowing feast effect.

TIPS

Encourage your guests to make little open-faced sandwiches topped with pickled cranberries for a burst of flavor. The pumpkin butter borders on a sweet spread, so for a more savory board, you could replace it with a trio of mustards.

Bourbon Pumpkin Butter (page 160)
Mashed Potato Dip (page 144)
Pickled Cranberries (page 170)

Green globe grapes, 3 cups
Brussels sprouts, 8
Green and yellow string beans, 32
Radicchio, 1 small head
Assorted radishes, 1 bunch, greens attached

Speck, 20 slices
Barbecue roast turkey, 16 large slices

Spiced-cumin Gouda, 9 oz
Farm-style aged Cheddar, 7 oz
Semisoft artisan amber-ale Cheddar, 7 oz
Garlic and rosemary chèvre, 5 oz

Miniature dinner buns, 24

Edible flowers, for garnish
Miniature gourds or pears, for garnish

CHRISTMAS DINNER ON A BOARD

 Enjoy this with a white Christmas sangria complete with cranberries and a rosemary sprig.

Before we became parents, as working professionals, we opted out of a traditional family Christmas dinner in favor of something more intimate with friends. This board has all the elements of a Christmas dinner—slow-roasted beef bought thinly shaved from the butcher, honey-drizzled carrots and beet salad on a stick—but without the big production. It works as a centerpiece for a potluck-style gathering or as the main event the night before St. Nick arrives.

PREPARATION

Make the Cherry Cabernet Relish and Cranberry Mustard. Serve in bowls.

Leave 1″ of greens on the carrots and slice them into long spears.

Prepare a beet salad on a stick: Measure about 1 Tbsp of the hazelnuts into a small resealable plastic bag. With a heavy-bottomed glass, crush the hazelnuts into a fine crumb. Pour the crushed nuts onto a small plate and mix in the ground pepper. Take about 1/4 oz of the chèvre and roll it into a small ball, then roll it in the nut mixture. Set aside and repeat with the remaining chèvre until you make 8 balls. Slice the beets in half. Slide a beet half onto a decorative toothpick, followed by spinach leaves and a chèvre ball.

Slice the baguette into 1/2″ slices.

Serve all the other components in the style that works best for you (see page 23 for tips), then arrange everything on and around your board. Top with optional garnishes.

TIPS

If prime rib is on your Christmas menu, you can make this board for Boxing Day lunch with the leftovers. Some striking flavor combinations here are bread, Cherry Cabernet Relish, herbed cheese and rare beef; bread, Cranberry Mustard, garlic roast beef and apricot Stilton; roast beef wrapped around blue cheese, a cornichon and a carrot; and bread, a goat cheese ball and hazelnuts.

Cherry Cabernet Relish (page 157)
Cranberry Mustard (page 157)

Carrots, 8, greens attached
Canned beets, 4
Spinach, 32 leaves

Herbed roast beef, 24 slices
Garlic roast beef, 16 slices

Herbed Havarti cheese, 8 oz
White Stilton with apricot, 6 oz
Blue cheese, 4 oz
Chèvre, 2 oz

Baguette, 1

Hazelnuts, 1/2 cup
Coarse ground black pepper, 1/2 tsp

Assorted olives, 10
Cornichons, 1/3 cup

Fresh rosemary, for garnish
Pear, for garnish

DREAMING OF A WHITE CHRISTMAS

SERVES 8

An oaky, buttery Chardonnay is a nice alternative to the traditional reds of the season and will bring out the nuttiness of the creamy Bries.

Most of the boards in this book do not include anything hot. The whole point is to be able to prep everything before your guests arrive so you can spend more time with them and less time in the kitchen. But this board is an exception because nothing says holidays like a baked Brie. So much so that this board has two. Each brie could stand alone, but together they're a showstopper. The added beauty is that they can still be prepared in advance and simply removed from the oven when you're ready to serve. Pistachios, pecans and pomegranate arils are prominent Christmas flavors and pair beautifully with the Bries.

PREPARATION

Prepare the fruit: Snip the grapes into clusters of 4 to 6. Last minute: Core the apples and use a mandoline or sharp knife to slice them.

Prepare the roast garlic: Preheat the oven to 375°F. Slice the top off each garlic bulb so the tips of the cloves are visible. Drizzle the tops of the cloves with the olive oil, wrap each bulb tightly in aluminum foil and roast for about 40 minutes. Bulbs can be served warm or cold.

Prepare the two different Bries: Top each Brie with its respective flavors and place each in an ovenproof serving dish (see tip). Just before serving, place in a 375°F oven and warm for about 15 minutes. You could also add them to the oven when the garlic is baking for the final 15 minutes. If you like, reserve some of each of the nuts to serve on their own in a small bowl.

Slice the baguette into ¼″ slices and toast it.

Serve the other components in the style that works best for you (see page 23 for tips), then arrange everything on and around your board.

TIPS

A small cast-iron pan is perfect for baking a Brie and looks great on a board. Just remember to put a trivet or coaster underneath if the pan is still hot. Some Bries come in their own baking dish, which can go directly onto the board.

For an ooey-gooey dish, consider removing the top rind of the Brie before adding the toppings and baking; instead of slicing, your guests can scoop into the melty goodness. See page 15 for tips on cutting Brie.

Green grapes, 3 cups
Green apple, 1
Red apple, 1
Garlic, 3 bulbs
Extra virgin olive oil, 2 Tbsp

Parmesan-rind salami, 24 slices
Chorizo salami, 16 slices

Double-crème Brie, 10 oz
Pecans, 12
Cranberries, 12
Blackberries, 8
Fresh thyme, 2 sprigs
Bloomy-rind Brie, 7 oz
Pistachios, shelled, ½ cup
Pomegranate arils, ¼ cup
Fresh rosemary, chopped, 2 Tbsp

Baguette, 1

HAPPY NEW YEAR!

SERVES 8

🥂 Keep the Champagne flowing all night long.

Champagne wishes and caviar dreams! There really is no better accompaniment to Champagne than this luxurious caviar board, featuring three different types of caviar. On a night when everyone is dressed to the nines, you want to keep the food elegant and simple. Everything can be prepped ahead, but don't bring the caviar out until just before midnight. It's best consumed within an hour of opening, so have everything else ready, crack the jars and serve on ice.

PREPARATION

Make the Quick Pickled Onions and serve in a small bowl.

Prepare the fruit and vegetables: Snip the grapes into clusters of 4 to 6. Cut the lemon into 8 wedges. Using a mandoline or very sharp knife, slice the cucumber at a slight angle to achieve oval-shaped pieces. Finely mince the red onion.

Lox usually comes sliced, so separate each piece and then gently pile up on the board and garnish with dill. The caviar should be served ice-cold and on ice. Serve them directly in their containers on a bowl of ice (shaved or crushed mold better, but melt faster) or a frozen Himalayan salt block.

Serve the minced red onion, capers and crème fraîche in small bowls. Lay out the other components in the style that works best for you (see page 23 for tips).

TIPS

Never use metal spoons with caviar (the metal reacts negatively with the eggs). If you don't have a mother-of-pearl spoon, a small wooden or glass one will work great. Caviar can be incredibly expensive (beluga being one of the priciest), but there are some reasonably priced varieties. I prefer to offer a range of mid-priced caviars of varying colors, size and flavors, but you could also go with one showstopper. Also, a little goes a long way. Because most people are not familiar with caviar, create a few starter toasts to show your guests how much they need.

Quick Pickled Onions (page 168)

Black grapes, 4 cups
Lemon, 1
English cucumber, 1 large
Red onion, ½

Wild Alaskan lox, 1 lb
Salmon caviar, 4 oz
Red lumpfish caviar, 4 oz
Sturgeon caviar, 4 oz

Mini toast crackers, 36

Capers, ½ cup
Crème fraîche, ½ cup
Fresh dill, for garnish

Around the World

BOARDS

OH, CANADA

SERVES 4

Oh, Canada! Presenting the cultural mosaic of my native Canada on one small board proved challenging. The country's vast land mass and diverse growing climates mean you almost need a board equally as vast to do justice to the culinary range. While maple syrup and poutine may be some of the foods that come to mind, Canada produces many culinary treats beyond these stereotypes. Cheddar, semisoft and goat cheeses are all readily available from both large and small producers; maple back bacon and candied salmon come courtesy of the farming and fishing industries; and Canadian wines are starting to be recognized internationally.

PREPARATION

Fry the back bacon according to package instructions. During the final minute of cooking, drizzle both sides with the maple syrup and allow it to caramelize on the bacon.

Slice the baguette into ¼″ slices and toast it.

Last minute: Using a mandoline, slice the apples into very thin wedges. If preparing in advance, store the apples in water with some lemon juice to prevent them from oxidizing.

Serve the other components in the style that works best for you (see page 23 for tips), then arrange everything on and around your board. Top with optional garnishes.

TIPS

There are many Canadian foods not represented on this board that easily could be. From East Coast lobster, to Montreal smoked beef, to the breads and bannocks of Indigenous communities, the breadth and depth of culinary options in this country are almost overwhelming. So where do you start? Wherever you are in Canada, choose local and in season and you won't go wrong.

Green apple, ½
Red apple, ½
Assorted berries (strawberries,
    blackberries, raspberries,
    blueberries), 1½ cups
Green and yellow string beans, 8

Back bacon, 8 slices
Maple syrup (grade A amber), 2 Tbsp
Double-smoked sockeye salmon, 8 oz

Smoked Oka cheese, 6 oz
Canadian Brie, 6 oz

Baguette, ½

Walnuts, 8 shelled
Dried blueberries, 2 Tbsp

Fresh dill, for garnish
Pattypan squash, for garnish

RED, WHITE & BLUE

SERVES 4

When you're trying to make a board that represents a country as broad and diverse as the United States, where do you even start? American cuisine is influenced by so many different cultures and geographies. To honor the nation, this board starts with a flag made from beautiful West Coast produce and cheese, and ends on the East Coast with pastrami and pickles. In between, taste the flavors of the Midwest with corn on the cob and wild game charcuterie, and round it out with creamy Southern pimento dip and bourbon bacon jam.

PREPARATION

Make the Kentucky Bourbon Bacon Jam and Caviar of the South. Serve in jars on the board.

Boil the corn for 6 to 8 minutes, or until tender and bright yellow. Cut the cobs into about 3" pieces. Cut each skewer into about 3 to 4 pieces, then insert a piece of skewer into the corn on the cob to make a handle.

Make an American flag of bocconcini skewers: Thread 4 small wooden skewers with alternating bocconcini and tomatoes, using 3 tomatoes and 2 pieces of cheese per stick. On another 4 small skewers, place 4 blueberries, then 1 tomato, 1 bocconcini and 1 final tomato. When laid out in the corner of the board, it should resemble the American flag.

Slice the baguette.

Serve the other components in the style that best for you (see page 23 for tips), then arrange everything on and around your board. Top with optional garnishes.

TIPS

There are so many possible variations for this board, especially if you focus on one specific region. A West Coast board could feature a variety of smoked and cured Pacific Ocean fish, complemented with the bounty of fresh fruits and vegetables from California. Or take a trip down South and serve crawfish dip, hush puppies and a bite-size version of chicken and waffles.

Kentucky Bourbon Bacon Jam
   (page 158)
Caviar of the South (page 170)

Watermelon, 4 slices
Blueberries, 16
Corn on the cob, 2 medium cobs
Grape tomatoes, 20

Wild boar salami, 1 link
Pastrami, 8 slices
Bison jerky, 8 small pieces

Bocconcini, 12 small balls

Rice crackers, 16
Baguette, ½ loaf
Pretzels, 1 cup

Mustard pickles, ⅓ cup
Dried oranges, 5 slices

Pea shoots, for garnish
Sunflower, for garnish

MEXICAN FIESTA

SERVES 4

Two great options for carrying the Mexican theme into the evening are a build-your-own taco bar and a baked dish of enchiladas.

You can't go wrong with a pitcher of lime margaritas or a bucket of ice-cold *cervezas*.

Cinco de Mayo. Margarita Monday. Taco Tuesday. There is no shortage of reasons to celebrate the flavors of Mexican food. A Mexican board is a great opportunity to abandon the go-to heaping plate of nachos in favor of a sort of deconstructed board. Mexico has some beautiful quesos—cheeses in Spanish—that have become more accessible at mainstream grocers. For this board, I swap out the usual crackers or bread for more authentic dipping vehicles— corn tostadas and colorful tortillas. And the street food–style corn elote is converted into a simple but impressive dip.

PREPARATION

Make the Elote Dip and Pico de Gallo. Serve in bowls on the board.

Prepare the fruit and vegetables: Snip the tomatoes into clusters of 2 to 4. Slice the limes into small wedges. Slice the jalapeño into thin slices. Cut most of the stems off the cilantro and break it into 3- to 6-leaf pieces. Last minute: Slice 1 avocado in half and the other into wedges. Squeeze some of the lime juice over the avocados and elote dip for a burst of freshness (and maybe save one for your margarita).

Slice the chorizo into bite-size pieces.

Slice the tostadas into quarter triangles.

Fold down the tops of three brown paper bags (lunch-bag size) about a third of the way. Fill each one with different colored tortilla chips.

Fill a ramekin flush with the sour cream and, using a butter knife, level it off flat.

Serve the other components in the style that works best for you (see page 23 for tips), then arrange everything, fiesta style, on and around your board.

TIPS

Mexican chorizo can be difficult to find and is usually sold raw. Its close counterpart, cured Spanish chorizo, is readily available in the deli section of most grocers and makes for a great substitute. Pepitas are also sold as pumpkin seeds and can be purchased in most grocery stores.

Elote Dip (Mexican Street Corn) (page 145)
Pico de Gallo (page 145)

Cherry tomatoes on the vine, 16
Limes, 2
Avocados, 2 large
Jalapeño, 1 large
Fresh cilantro, 1/3 cup

Chorizo sausages, cooked or cured, 4 (14 oz total)

Oaxaca cheese, 7 oz
Manchego cheese, 5 oz

Corn tostadas, 12
White corn, blue corn and red corn tortilla chips, 5 cups each

Sour cream, 1/3 cup
Pumpkin seeds (pepitas), 1/4 cup

BARCELONA ON A BOARD

SERVES 8

For a showstopper of a night, serve a massive seafood paella family-style.

 Whip up a red or white sangria with fruit in season.

Spanish food is made for gathering. Whether it be tapas bites or a pan of paella, Spanish food is designed to bring people together over a shared experience. Three cheeses—including the popular Drunken Goat—represent three distinct regions of Spain. A Spanish board would also not be complete without a spoon of quince paste for sweetness, a dish of olives for brine and the famous Spanish nut—the Marcona almond—for a rich crunch.

PREPARATION

Make the Romesco Sauce and serve in a bowl.

Prepare the dates: Make a small incision in each date, remove the pit and stuff each date with 1 Tbsp Cabrales cheese.

Slice about 1½ of the chorizo links into ¼" slices, leaving at least 1 link whole for the board.

In a small bowl, toss the almonds with the smoked paprika and serve scattered around the board

Slice the bread into ½" slices.

Prepare the other components in the style that works best for you (see page 23 for tips), then arrange everything on and around your board. Top with optional garnishes.

TIPS

Romesco sauce is a classic Spanish dip made with roasted red peppers. It is addictively good and can be used as a pasta sauce or spooned over grilled chicken. Consider doubling the recipe and freezing the extra for another meal.

Other beautiful combinations on this board are a blue cheese–stuffed date wrapped in a small piece of serrano; bread topped with a slice of Manchego and a dollop of quince paste; and a thin slice of Drunken Goat and a schmear of romesco atop a slice of bread.

Romesco Sauce (page 150)

Black and green grapes on the vine, 4 cups total

Dates, 8

Chorizo, cured, 3 links
Serrano ham, 16 very thin slices

Drunken Goat cheese, 5 oz
Manchego cheese, 6 oz
Iberico cheese, 5 oz
Cabrales cheese, 8 Tbsp (3 oz)

Mixed olives, ¾ cup
Marcona almonds, ⅓ cup
Pimentón (Spanish smoked paprika), 1 Tbsp
Quince paste, ¼ cup

Crusty bread, 1 long loaf

Fresh figs, for garnish
Pea shoots, for garnish

BAGUETTES, BRIES & BERETS

SERVES 4

 A bottle of Côtes du Rhône is the perfect pairing for this board.

There is something about dining outdoors with a glass of wine and a torn piece of baguette that feels so French countryside. There is more space on this board, but the composition of each bite will leave your guests feeling anything but empty. Restraint is actually the most difficult part of composing this board—it's quality over quantity—so go ahead and splurge on the best ingredients. The French take their cheese—and how to slice it—very seriously. I highly recommend you take another look at page 15 for a primer on how to properly cut a piece of cheese.

PREPARATION

Make the Butter-Dipped Radishes and Wine-Soaked Blackberries. Serve the radishes directly on the board and use the blackberries to top the Brie (see below).

If the pâté comes in a log or slice form, consider scooping it into a small mason jar for easy access to the perfect schmear.

Remove the Brie from its packaging, and using a slotted spoon, gently place some blackberries on top. Getting a little of their wine on the Brie is a good thing, but you don't want to soak it. Slice one of the figs in half lengthwise and place on top of the Brie.

Serve the other components in the style that works best for you (see page 23 for tips), then arrange everything on and around your board.

TIP

Two flavor combinations to get your guests started are a small slice of Brie topped with a blackberry and a few flakes of salt, and a schmear of pâté topped with a piece of cornichon.

Butter-Dipped Radishes (page 164)
Wine-Soaked Blackberries (page 179)

Fresh figs, 2

Chicken liver pâté, 8 oz
Saucisson sec (salami), 16 slices

Double-crème Brie, 1 round
Comté, 8 oz

Picholine olives, 4
Cornichons, 4

Baguette, 1

POSTCARD FROM AMSTERDAM

SERVES 4

The Dutch take a very simple and straightforward approach to their cuisine, which most people probably associate with their most famous cheese: Gouda. Gouda is widely available in North America and comes in a multitude of varieties. It is very mild and creamy and can be found plain, smoked or flavored. This board uses two versions of Gouda plus an Edam, another popular Dutch cheese. Because these cheeses have similar textures, the vegetables on this board have a high crunch factor. The bread or crackers on the board represent kaas-stengels, *a traditional puff pastry twisted with cheese.*

PREPARATION

Prepare the vegetables: Wash the carrots and peel them if necessary, leaving the top 2" to 3" of greens attached. Scrub the white radishes and leave the top couple inches of greens attached. Cut the bottom stem away from the endive and gently remove each leaf.

Serve the other components in the style that works best for you (see page 23 for tips), then arrange everything on and around your board.

TIPS

This board would be a great starter to any meal, any time of day. If served as the beginning to a leisurely brunch, you could follow with *pannekoeken*, the traditional Dutch pancakes that can be eaten with sweet or savory accompaniments.

On a chilly fall day, serve this board with a warm bowl of thick pea soup—called *erwtensoep*—made from dried green split peas, pork and aromatics.

For dinner, serve this board with some *bitterballen* (a crusted, deep-fried meatball usually served with a selection of grainy, spicy mustards) to create a more rounded selection of savory snacks, or *bittergarnituur*, as the Dutch call them.

Carrots, 8 small, greens attached

White box radishes, 8, greens attached

Belgian endive, 1 small head

Smoked mackerel fillet, 8 oz

Smoked bratwurst, 2 links

European cooked ham, 8 thin slices

Double-cream Gouda, 6 oz

Herbed Gouda, 6 oz

Edam, 5 oz

Puffed cheese twists, 8

Microgreens, for garnish

Currants, for garnish

BAVARIAN BOUNTY

SERVES 8

This is a heavy meat and bread board. While schnitzel may be tempting, a big, bright salad or crudité platter would be a better option to complete this German meal.

Raise your glass and say *"prost"* with a dry German Riesling or a frosty Kölsch brew.

Break out your best lederhosen or dirndl! Whether you're celebrating Oktoberfest or just a Tuesday night, a German-themed board is a great excuse to drink beer and indulge in some sausages, pretzels and cheese. In fact, Germany is actually one of the top cheese producers in the world. If you have access to a German deli, head there first for some of the best selections of unique liverwursts, sausages and mustards. If you don't have one near you, don't worry, you can make this board from what you can find at your local grocer.

PREPARATION

Make the Beer Pretzel Dip and serve in a bowl on the board.

Wrap some of the pretzel sticks in pieces of the cervelat salami. Break the fresh pretzels into 2 or 3 pieces. Toast the rye bread and cut each slice in half.

Serve the other components in the style that works best for you (see page 23 for tips), then arrange everything on and around your board.

TIPS

Turn the evening into a tasting party! Line up some short glasses and pour readily available German pilsners and *hefeweizens* (wheat beer).

German chocolate is some of the best in the world. Create a small board with some different varieties alongside some sweet green grapes.

Beer Pretzel Dip (page 144)

Cherry tomatoes, 8

German fine liverwurst, 8 oz
Kalbs liverwurst, 8 oz
Cervelat salami, 24 slices
Black Forest ham, 16 slices
Schinkenspeck, 16 slices
Landjaeger, 2 links

Emmental, 12 oz
German Brie, 8 oz

Pretzel sticks, 2 cups
Fresh bread pretzels, 4 large
Rye bread, 5 thick slices

Sauerkraut, ⅓ cup
Cornichons, ⅓ cup
Assorted nuts, ⅓ cup
Mustard trio, 2 Tbsp each of yellow,
    Bavarian and Dijon

Fresh flat-leaf parsley, for garnish

MOUNTAIN OF SWISS FONDUE

SERVES 8

 Kirsch is traditional Swiss brandy that pairs well with a rich fondue.

In North America, fondue dates back to the 60s. It evolved to include broths, oils and even chocolate. In Switzerland, it's strictly a cheese dish originating as a hearty peasant meal that made use of the foods most readily available during the winter in the Alps—cheese, wine and bread. The addition of baby potatoes and sturdy Swiss chard stalks means this board will eat like a meal. With the weight of the bread and cheese, always serve contrast on this board; bright, crisp cornichons and plump, sweet grapes are welcome choices.

PREPARATION

Prepare the fruit and vegetables: Snip the grapes into clusters of 4 to 6. Slice the figs into halves or quarters. Last minute: Core the apple and use a mandoline or very sharp knife to thinly slice it.

Steam the potatoes until fork-tender (see page 59). Trim the leaves off the chard stalks and cut each into 2 long stalks.

Slice the French loaf into bite-size cubes.

Prepare the other components (except the cheese) in bite-sized pieces and arrange everything on and around your board (see page 23 for tips).

When you're ready to serve, melt the fondue cheese blend and Swiss cheese in a small pot over low heat and avoid stirring. When the cheese is fully melted, pour it into a fondue pot and light the flame or tealight. Retain any excess cheese on the stove off the heat and repeat the process to replenish as the fondue pot depletes.

TIPS

If you want to attempt a homemade cheese blend, you'll need a mix of Swiss and Gruyère, white wine, dry mustard and cornstarch to get you started. While the Swiss don't commonly fondue much more than cheese, you could easily turn this into a full-on fondue party by adding an oil or broth fondue and some raw proteins.

Black grapes, 3 cups
Fresh figs, 2
Green apple, 1
Baby potatoes, 24
Swiss chard, 8 stalks

Kielbasa, 12 oz ring
Dried chorizo sausage, 4 small links

Fondue cheese blend, 20 oz
Swiss cheese, 10 oz

French loaf or baguette, 1

Cornichons, 16
Pickled onions, 16

Fresh thyme, for garnish
Pea shoots, for garnish

LITTLE ITALY

SERVES 8

Look for a bottle of Chianti marked Classico—which indicates the grapes came from one of the original four villages that produced Chianti—or Riserva—meaning the wine has aged for at least 27 months.

I married an Italian, so there was a lot of pressure when I was designing this board! The best approach to creating an Italian board is to visit your local Italian deli. Politely ask the signora behind the counter for some mortadella and a special prosciutto—she'll know to slice it transparently thin. Select a burrata, a provolone and maybe a small piece of Parmesan. Swing by the olive bar, and don't forget the bread. The quality of these components is so great, you could just lay them on the counter and it would be heavenly. Salute!

PREPARATION

Prepare the fruit: Snip the grapes into clusters of 4 to 6. Slice the figs in half. Slice the cantaloupe into thin wedges (¼" to ½" thick), and wrap some of the wedges with half a slice of prosciutto.

Serve the pickled squid and giardiniera in small bowls. Prepare all the other components in the style that works best for you (see page 23 for tips), then arrange everything on and around your board, with the garnishes nestled in.

TIPS

This board calls for more olives than will likely be eaten, but the long olive dish makes for a dramatic presentation. As long as they're kept refrigerated in an airtight container, olives will keep in their brine for up to 1 month and out of the brine for up to 2 weeks.

Finocchiona, like many other hard Italian salamis, comes with a skin or peel. Whether to peel this skin off or eat it is heavily debated. My advice is to leave the skin on and let guests make their own choice. Some people find it chewy, while others feel it adds to the flavor.

Black grapes, 3 cups
Fresh figs, 4
Cantaloupe, ½

Prosciutto di Parma, 16 slices
Soppressata salami, hot, 16 slices
Mortadella, 16 slices
Bresaola, 16 slices
Finocchiona salami, 1 link

Provolone, 10 oz
Asiago, 10 oz
Burrata, 8 oz

Croccantini Italian crackers, 32

Pickled squid, ½ cup
Giardiniera (pickled vegetables), ½ cup
Assorted olives, 40 (see tips)

Small pears, for garnish
Fresh basil, for garnish

MEDITERRANEAN MEZZE

SERVES 8

This is a very hearty board. It could easily be made into a meal by simply adding some grilled souvlaki skewers and a side of tzatziki.

The Mediterranean diet—abundant in fruits, vegetables, legumes and olive oil—has been hailed as one of the healthiest in the world. The Greek culture does a tremendous job of bringing together contrasting profiles—creamy, crunchy, briny and sweet—for a never-ending choice of flavor combinations. This board is so rich not only in flavor but also in composition that it serves as a meal all on its own.

PREPARATION

Make the Basic Hummus and serve in a bowl on the board.

Prepare the vegetables: Peel the carrots, keeping about 2″ of the tops attached. Slice the cucumbers lengthwise into skinny strips. Last minute: Cut the avocado into wedges, leaving the peel on for easier handling.

Slice each pita into 8 triangles, like you'd slice a pie.

Serve the other components in the style that works best for you (see page 23 for tips), then arrange everything on and around your board. Top with optional garnish.

TIP

Short on time? Pick up some store-bought hummus and a can of chickpeas when you're picking up the dolmas, available at most grocers either canned or in the fresh deli department.

Basic Hummus (page 116)

Heirloom rainbow carrots, 16, greens attached
Tomatoes, 12, various sizes
English cucumbers, 2 small
Avocado, 1 large

Dry red-wine salami, 24 slices

Herbed feta cubes, 10 oz
Fresh mozzarella, 16 small balls

Pitas, 4

Dolmas, 10 oz
Halkidiki olives, 16

Blooming fresh oregano, for garnish

CHAAT & CHUTNEY

SERVES 4 (V)

 Kingfisher, the most popular Indian beer in North America, does a brilliant job of mellowing the heat of the chutneys.

In many parts of India, there is a vibrant food-cart scene that serves a wide range of snacks, often called chaat. These snacks are usually savory, like pieces of crisp flatbread topped with chutneys, sauces and spices. Indian food is one of our favorite takeaway choices, especially for a crowd, and this board is inspired by Indian street food, with three homemade condiments of vibrant color and flavor. It's a bright and fresh contrast to complement an evening full of rich kormas and dals.

PREPARATION

Make the Red Kashmir Chutney, Mint Green Chutney and Sunshine Mint Raita. Serve in bowls on the board.

Preheat the oven to 350°F.

Prepare the vegetables: Steam the cauliflower and potatoes separately until fork-tender (see page 59). Sprinkle the cauliflower with a mixture of 1 tsp of the smoked paprika, 1 tsp of the cumin and ½ tsp of the salt.

Prepare the paneer: Cut the paneer into equal bite-size cubes. To a small bowl, add 2 tsp each of chili powder, ground black pepper and garam masala, plus 1 tsp turmeric and 1 tsp of the salt. Mix the spices together and sprinkle over all sides of the paneer cubes. Add about 2 Tbsp oil to a shallow skillet and fry the paneer over medium-high heat until a brown crust forms.

Place the peanuts on a small baking sheet and sprinkle with 2 tsp of the smoked paprika and 1 tsp of the cumin. Roast in the oven for 10 minutes, turning once.

Prepare the pappadums: Heat about 1" of oil in a heavy skillet over medium-high heat. To test if the oil is hot enough, break off a tiny piece of pappadum and drop into the hot oil. If it sizzles right away, the oil is hot enough. Lay 1 pappadum wafer in the oil; it will puff up almost immediately. Flip it over with tongs and push it down into the oil. Once it is puffed and crisp (about 20 to 30 seconds), remove from the oil to a paper towel–lined plate. Break each pappadum into 2 to 3 pieces.

Arrange all of the components on and around your board (see page 23 for tips) topped with optional garnishes.

TIPS

The colorful condiments are the stars of this board, and they go beautifully with the potatoes. Be sure to put out small butter knives so people can cut the potatoes in half and experience the different flavors. Keep any pappadums that won't fit on the board in a sealed airtight bag. You can replenish the board partway through the evening if necessary.

Red Kashmir Chutney (page 156)
Mint Green Chutney (page 156)
Sunshine Mint Raita (page 152)

Cauliflower florets, 3 cups
Baby potatoes, 12

Paneer, 14 oz

Salted peanuts, 1 cup

Seasonings:
Chili powder, 2 tsp
Coarse ground black pepper, 2 tsp
Garam masala, 2 tsp
Ground turmeric, 1 tsp
Smoked paprika, 3 tsp
Ground cumin, 2 tsp
Flaked sea salt, 1½ tsp

Pappadums, 10
Vegetable oil, for frying

Fresh flat-leaf parsley, for garnish
Red chili, for garnish

LUNAR NEW YEAR FEAST

SERVES 4

 Pick up some wonton soup at your favorite takeout spot.

Living in a community with a large Chinese population, my family and I have become accustomed to celebrating Lunar New Year. This board is a fun and festive way to ring in the New Year, and to bridge the concept of a charcuterie board of the West with traditional flavors of the East. The main proteins are a salami speckled with orange rind and a rich duck prosciutto. The dim sum here is from my local Asian market, but you could certainly make your own. Alternatively, most major grocers carry a selection in their frozen foods department. If you are new to dim sum, start with prawn dumplings (har gow), *open-top pork dumplings* (siu mai) *or barbecue pork buns* (char siu bao).

PREPARATION

Make the Spicy Cold Tofu. Serve in a bowl on the board.

Prepare the vegetables: Drain the canned corn. Steam the Chinese long beans until tender-crisp, then transfer them to an ice bath. Drain and dry the beans, place them on a plate and sprinkle with sesame seeds. Using a mandoline or sharp knife, slice the green radish about 1/8" thick.

Boil the eggs for 2 minutes, then run them under cold water to cool. Leave them in their shells.

Prepare the dim sum according to package instructions.

Prepare the remaining components in the style that works best for you (see page 23 for tips), then arrange everything on and around your board.

TIP

If picking up dim sum, also select one of the barbecued ducks found in Asian supermarkets. Shred the duck and serve it alongside some fresh buns (Chinese bakeries have the most luxurious breads!) and a mixture of sriracha and mayonnaise for a DIY sandwich bar.

Spicy Cold Tofu (page 165)

Baby corn, 8 oz can

Chinese long beans, 8

Black and white sesame seeds, 1 Tbsp total

Chinese green radish, 1 medium

Duck prosciutto, 12 slices

Orange confit salami, 16 slices

Black sesame rice crackers, 20

Quail eggs, 4

Dim sum, 8 pieces

SUSHI & SAKE

SERVES 4

 Order a large sushi party tray! Add a crisp, cold sunomono salad as a refreshing palate cleanser.

 Japanese beer is generally mild and easy drinking, but sake is really the way to go!

Sushi makes a great impromptu entertaining meal because, without any fuss, it is already beautiful. We always order a variety of cooked and raw options so there is something for everyone. Dairy does not play a big role in the Japanese food culture, so for this board, the typical meat and cheese platter of North American design is replaced with lox and soft tofu.

PREPARATION

Make the Wasabi Edamame Dip and Hiyayakko Tofu. Serve in small dishes on the board.

Prepare the vegetables: Using the ribbon blade of a spiral-izer (or a mandoline or very sharp knife), cut the cucumbers into long, wide strips. Follow the cooking instructions for the edamame and serve cold. Last minute: Using a regular spiralizer blade, a mandoline or a very sharp knife, slice the beets.

Roll about 2 Tbsp cooked and cooled rice into a ball to make *onigiri* (rice balls). You may need to squeeze the rice to get it to hold together. Roll the rice in the black and white sesame seeds.

Arrange all of the components on and around your board (see page 23 for tips).

TIPS

You can stuff the *onigiri* with smoked fish or vegetables and add granulated garlic, dried onion or red pepper flakes to the sesame seeds. If you can't find pickled ginger at your local grocer, ask for extra when you're getting takeout. And when you're ordering sushi for takeout, bring your own boards to the restaurant. Ask them to plate the sushi on your serving dishes.

Wasabi Edamame Dip (page 152)
Hiyayakko Tofu (page 165)

English cucumbers, 2 small
Edamame beans, in the shell, 2 cups
Yellow beet, 1 medium

Lox, any type, 6 oz

Short-grain rice, cooked and cooled,
    2 cups
Black and white sesame seeds, ½ cup
    total
Rice crackers, 30

Pickled ginger, ¼ cup

WORLD FLAVORS

SERVES 4

 Singha is a readily available Thai beer that's perfect for this board.

One of the wonderful things about food is the way it unites people across all borders in a universal expression of love and thoughtfulness. This board is a perfect example: it pulls flavors from all over the world into something cohesive, delicious and beautiful. In this East meets West display, dried fruit and fried wonton wrappers sit alongside fresh vegetables and cheeses. Spicy Thai relish is paired with creamy Greek yogurt. Add some salty Italian meats, and this board is perfect for any crowd or occasion.

PREPARATION

Make the Spicy Thai Relish over Creamy Yogurt and serve in a bowl on the board.

Prepare the fruit and vegetables: Cut the lime into quarters. Blanch the beans, drizzle them with 1 Tbsp of the Thai chili sauce and sprinkle with salt to taste. Leave 1" of greens on the carrots. If the carrots are small enough, leave them whole; otherwise, slice them lengthwise. Using a mandoline or sharp knife, cut the radish into ⅛" slices. Cut the cucumber on an angle to create an oval shape.

Drizzle the remaining Thai chili sauce over the chèvre.

Prepare the wontons: Heat about 1" of oil in a Dutch oven over medium-high heat. To test if the oil is hot enough, break off a very small piece of wonton and drop it into the oil. If it sizzles immediately, the oil is ready. Gently slide the wonton wrappers into the oil 1 at a time, frying batches of 3 to 4 at a time depending on the size of your pan. (Don't overcrowd the pot.) Fry until crisp, about 20 seconds, then transfer to a paper towel–lined baking sheet to cool. Break them into random cracker-size shapes and season with salt.

Prepare the remaining components in the way that works best for you (see page 23 for tips), then arrange them on and around your board.

Spicy Thai Relish over Creamy Yogurt
(page 155)

Lime, 1
Green string beans, 16
Snap peas, 16
Rainbow carrots, 8, greens attached
Green radish, 1
English cucumber, 1

Capocollo, 16 slices

Chèvre, 4 oz

Wonton wrappers, 24
Vegetable oil, for frying
Sweet Thai chili sauce, ¼ cup
Flaked sea salt

Dried mango and papaya, 8 pieces
total

Red Thai chilies, for garnish
Thai basil, for garnish

THE RECIPES

Muhammara Dip & Dukkah Spiced Yogurt Dip (p. 140)

Dips & Sauces

MUHAMMARA DIP

(POWERED BY PLANTS, PAGE 55) — MAKES 1 ½ CUPS   (V)

Preheat the oven to 400°F. Spread the walnuts and bread crumbs on a baking sheet and roast for 5 minutes or until they're slightly brown. Keep a close eye so they don't burn.

Place the drained red peppers, olive oil, lemon juice, pomegranate molasses, red pepper flakes, cumin and salt in a food processor. Process until smooth, then add the walnuts and bread crumbs. Pulse until everything is well combined and the mixture has a dip-like consistency.

Keep the dip in an airtight container in the fridge for up to 5 days.

NOTE: This can be served immediately but will benefit from being in the fridge for a few hours or overnight. This helps the flavors come together and intensify more, resulting in an *extra* delicious dip.

1 cup walnuts, chopped
¼ cup dry bread crumbs
1 (12 oz) jar roasted red bell peppers, drained
3 Tbsp extra virgin olive oil
1 Tbsp lemon juice
1 Tbsp pomegranate molasses
1 tsp red pepper flakes
½ tsp ground cumin
½ tsp flaked sea salt

DUKKAH SPICED YOGURT DIP

(EAT YOUR VEGGIES, PAGE 57) — MAKES 1 CUP (V)

¼ cup shelled pistachios

¼ cup walnuts, shelled and roughly chopped

2 tsp white sesame seeds

1 tsp black sesame seeds

½ tsp cumin seeds

½ tsp caraway seeds

½ tsp flaked sea salt

1 cup full-fat plain Greek-style yogurt

1 tsp lemon juice

½ tsp extra virgin olive oil

To make the dukkah spice, heat a dry nonstick skillet over medium heat. Add the pistachios and walnuts, occasionally shaking the pan to keep them moving. When they become fragrant (about 3 minutes), add the sesame seeds, cumin seeds and caraway seeds and toast for another 2 minutes, constantly moving the skillet.

Transfer the seeds and nuts to a plate to cool. Once cool, combine with the flaked sea salt and crush with a mortar and pestle (or in a small food processor). You want the consistency of a crumble, not a paste, for the dukkah. Set aside.

In a small dish, combine the yogurt, lemon juice and 2 Tbsp dukkah. Top the yogurt with another 1 Tbsp dukkah and the olive oil. Keep the leftover dukkah spice in an airtight container in the fridge for up to 3 months.

NOTE: *Dukkah* is Egyptian Arabic and means "to pound." Feel free to experiment with different nut, seed and spice combinations.

GREEN GODDESS DIP

(EAT YOUR VEGGIES, PAGE 57) — MAKES 1 ¾ CUPS (V)

¼ cup chopped fresh flat-leaf parsley

¼ cup fresh basil, chopped

2 Tbsp fresh chives, chopped

1 small clove garlic

2 small ripe avocados

½ cup full-fat plain Greek-style yogurt

¼ cup full-fat mayonnaise

1 Tbsp lemon juice

1 tsp granulated sugar

1 tsp flaked sea salt

Place the parsley, basil, chives and garlic in a food processor or high-powered blender. Pulse just until everything is minced fine.

Roughly chop the avocados and add them to the food processor with the yogurt, mayonnaise, lemon juice, sugar and salt. Blend until completely smooth and creamy.

Keep in an airtight container in the fridge for up to 3 days.

HERBED YOGURT DIP

(BRIGHT & BLOOMING, PAGE 71) — MAKES 1 CUP   (V)

Place all the ingredients in a medium-size bowl and mix gently until well combined.

Keep in an airtight container in the fridge for up to 3 days.

NOTE: If the dip is too tangy or not quite thick enough, add up to a ½ cup of full-fat sour cream, 1 Tbsp at a time, until it's just right for your needs.

1 cup full-fat plain Greek-style yogurt
2 Tbsp chopped fresh flat-leaf
    parsley leaves
1 Tbsp chopped fresh dill
1 Tbsp chopped fresh chives
1 Tbsp chopped fresh mint leaves
1 tsp lemon juice
1 tsp lemon zest
½ tsp flaked sea salt

WEDGE SALAD DIP

(GAME-DAY SNACK STADIUM, PAGE 95)   — MAKES 4 CUPS

Place the sour cream, cream cheese and all of the seasonings in a medium bowl and mix with a wooden spoon until well combined.

Fold in the lettuce, bacon and blue cheese.

Top with the reserved lettuce and bacon.

Refrigerate for 1 hour before serving. This dip does not store well, as the lettuce goes soggy. To keep this dip longer, add the lettuce to just the portion you think will be consumed. The dip without the lettuce can be stored in an airtight container in the fridge for up to 5 days.

1 cup full-fat sour cream
1 cup full-fat cream cheese, room
    temperature
2 tsp dried parsley
2 tsp dried dill
2 tsp onion powder
2 tsp flaked sea salt
1 tsp garlic powder
¼ tsp coarse ground black pepper
1½ cups chopped iceberg lettuce,
    2 Tbsp reserved
¾ cup cooked bacon, 1 Tbsp
    reserved
½ cup crumbled blue cheese

*Wedge Salad (p. 141), Buffalo Chicken, Beer Pretzel (p. 144)
& Mashed Potato (p. 144) Dips*

BUFFALO CHICKEN DIP

(GAME-DAY SNACK STADIUM, PAGE 95) — MAKES 3 CUPS

Place all the ingredients in a large bowl and mix by hand until everything is well incorporated.

Scoop into a serving bowl, cover with plastic wrap and let set in the fridge for an hour before serving.

Keep this in an airtight container in the fridge for up to 3 days. This recipe can be easily halved for smaller gatherings.

NOTES: A cooked rotisserie chicken from the grocery deli department is great for this recipe, as you can use both white and dark meat. Whipped cream cheese can be used in place of the cream cheese for a slightly lighter texture.

2 cups shredded cooked chicken (see notes)

1 cup full-fat cream cheese, room temperature (see notes)

½ cup of your favorite cayenne pepper sauce

¼ cup finely chopped fresh chives

1 tsp onion powder

½ tsp garlic powder

RANCH DIP

(NO GROWN UPS ALLOWED, PAGE 41) — MAKES 1 CUP   (V)

In a small bowl, combine the mayonnaise, sour cream, onion powder, garlic powder and salt.

Gently add the parsley and chives and stir until well combined.

Transfer to a serving bowl and garnish with a fresh parsley leaf.

Keep this in an airtight container in the fridge for up to 7 days.

NOTE: The flavor of the dip will benefit from 4 hours to overnight in the fridge.

⅔ cup full-fat mayonnaise

⅓ cup full-fat sour cream

1 tsp onion powder

½ tsp garlic powder

½ tsp flaked sea salt

2 Tbsp minced fresh flat-leaf parsley, plus 1 leaf for garnish

1 Tbsp minced fresh chives

BEER PRETZEL DIP

(BAVARIAN BOUNTY, PAGE 121) — MAKES 3 ½ CUPS (V)

2 cups full-fat cream cheese, cubed
and at room temperature

1½ cups shredded aged white
Cheddar

3 tsp onion powder

2 tsp garlic powder

½ tsp coarse ground black pepper

6 oz beer (see note)

⅓ cup chopped fresh chives

In a medium bowl, mix the cream cheese, Cheddar and dry seasonings with a wooden spoon until well creamy and well combined.

Stir in the beer. Fold in the chives.

Let stand in the fridge, covered, for at least 1 hour before serving.

Keep this in an airtight container in the fridge for up to 3 days. This recipe can be easily halved for smaller gatherings.

NOTE: The darker the beer, the stronger the flavor.

MASHED POTATO DIP

(THANKSGIVING FEAST, PAGE 99) — MAKES 1 ¾ CUPS

½ cup mashed potatoes (1 medium
potato), room temperature

⅓ cup full-fat sour cream

⅓ cup full-fat mayonnaise

1 tsp flaked sea salt

1 tsp onion powder

½ tsp garlic powder

⅓ cup chopped scallions (white and
green parts), 1 Tbsp reserved

⅓ cup crumbled cooked bacon,
1 Tbsp reserved

Place the potatoes, sour cream, mayonnaise and seasonings in a food processor. Blend until smooth, but do not overprocess.

Fold in the scallions and cooked bacon. Transfer to a serving bowl and sprinkle the reserved scallions and bacon over top.

Serve right away or refrigerate in an airtight container for up to 3 days. Remove from the fridge 1 hour before serving.

ELOTE DIP (MEXICAN STREET CORN)

(MEXICAN FIESTA, PAGE 112) — MAKES 2 CUPS (V)

In a cast-iron or heavy-bottomed skillet, heat the oil over medium heat.

Add the corn kernels and spread them out so they're covering the entire surface area of the pan. Let cook, without stirring or touching, for 2 minutes or until some of the kernels get some char, then toss them around the skillet for another minute. Remove from heat and pour into a medium-size bowl.

Add the cheese, lime juice, chili powder and salt and stir until well combined.

Add the cilantro leaves and toss gently.

Serve immediately or cover with plastic wrap and chill for at least 2 hours before serving.

Keep this in an airtight container in the fridge for up to 3 days.

1 Tbsp extra virgin olive oil
2 cups peaches-and-cream corn kernels (canned or off the cob)
2 Tbsp crumbled feta or cotija cheese
2 Tbsp lime juice
1 Tbsp chili powder
1 tsp flaked sea salt
2 Tbsp chopped fresh cilantro leaves

PICO DE GALLO

(MEXICAN FIESTA, PAGE 112) — MAKES 1½ CUPS (V)

Place all the ingredients in a medium-size bowl.

Toss gently until well combined.

Serve immediately or chill for an hour or so before serving, if you prefer. Keep in an airtight container in the fridge for up to 3 days.

5 Roma tomatoes, chopped
1 clove garlic, finely minced
⅓ cup diced Walla Walla or white onion
⅓ cup chopped fresh cilantro leaves
2 Tbsp lime juice
1 Tbsp finely minced jalapeño, seeds removed
1 tsp flaked sea salt

BASIC HUMMUS

(MEDITERRANEAN MEZZE, PAGE 127) —— MAKES 1 ½ CUPS (V)

2 Tbsp tahini

1 clove garlic, minced

1 Tbsp lemon juice

4 Tbsp extra virgin olive oil, divided

1 tsp flaked sea salt

1½ cups canned chickpeas, rinsed, drained and skins removed (see note)

Using a food processor, blend together the tahini, garlic and lemon juice until very creamy and smooth, scraping down the sides of the processor as necessary.

Add 3 Tbsp olive oil, the salt and half of the chickpeas. Process for about 1 minute until they just start to break down, scraping down the sides of the processor as necessary. Add the remaining chickpeas and process for 1 minute. Add 1 to 2 tsp water as needed to achieve an ultra-smooth, creamy texture.

Scoop the hummus into a bowl and drizzle with the remaining 1 Tbsp olive oil.

Keep in an airtight container in the fridge for up to 7 days.

NOTE: Removing the skins of the chickpeas is optional, but doing so produces a far superior, creamy hummus.

BEET HUMMUS

(TRIO OF HUMMUS, PAGE 52) —— MAKES 2 CUPS (V)

1 clove garlic, minced

2 Tbsp lemon juice

1 Tbsp tahini

1 cup grated cooked beets

2 Tbsp extra virgin olive oil, plus 1 tsp for drizzling

1 tsp flaked sea salt

1 cup canned chickpeas, rinsed, drained and skins removed (see note above)

In a food processor, blend together the garlic, lemon juice and tahini until very creamy and smooth, scraping down the sides of the processor as necessary.

Add the beets, 2 Tbsp olive oil and the salt. Process for about 1 minute, again scraping down the sides as necessary.

Add half of the chickpeas and process for 1 minute until they just start to break down. Add the remaining chickpeas and process for another 1 to 2 minutes. Add 1 to 2 tsp water as needed to achieve an ultra-smooth, creamy texture.

Scoop the hummus into a bowl and drizzle with the remaining olive oil.

Keep in an airtight container in the fridge for up to 7 days.

NOTE: Pickled beets are not suitable for this recipe.

Dips & Sauces

Basic, Butternut Squash, Beet, Green & Golden Hummus (p. 146–149)

BUTTERNUT SQUASH HUMMUS

(VEGETABLE HARVEST, PAGE 77) — MAKES 2 ½ CUPS (V)

1 cup cubed butternut squash

¼ cup + 1 Tbsp extra virgin olive oil

1 (15 oz) can chickpeas, rinsed, drained and skins removed (see note, page 146)

2 cloves garlic

⅓ cup tahini

1 Tbsp lemon juice

1 tsp flaked sea salt

1 tsp sweet paprika

¼ tsp ground sage

Preheat the oven to 400°F. Arrange the butternut squash on a baking sheet and drizzle with the 1 Tbsp olive oil. Roast until fork-tender, about 15 minutes.

While the squash is roasting, place the remaining ingredients in a food processor. Once the squash is tender, add it to the processor. Puree until silky smooth, adding water ½ tsp at a time until it reaches your desired consistency.

Keep in an airtight container in the fridge for up to 7 days.

GOLDEN HUMMUS

(TRIO OF HUMMUS , PAGE 52) — MAKES 1 ½ CUPS (V)

2 Tbsp tahini

1 clove garlic, minced

1 Tbsp lemon juice

3 Tbsp extra virgin olive oil, plus 1 tsp for drizzling

1 Tbsp ground turmeric

1 tsp sweet paprika

1 tsp flaked sea salt

1½ cups canned chickpeas, rinsed, drained and skins removed (see note, page 146)

In a food processor, blend together the tahini, garlic and lemon juice until very creamy and smooth, scraping down the sides of the processor as necessary.

Add the 3 Tbsp olive oil, turmeric, paprika and salt. Process for about 1 minute, again scraping down the sides as necessary.

Add half of the chickpeas and process for 1 minute until they just start to break down. Add the remaining chickpeas and process for another 1 to 2 minutes. Add 1 to 2 tsp water as needed to achieve an ultra-smooth, creamy texture.

Scoop the hummus into a bowl and drizzle with the remaining 1 tsp olive oil.

Keep in an airtight container in the fridge for up to 7 days.

GREEN HUMMUS

(TRIO OF HUMMUS , PAGE 52) — MAKES 1 ½ CUPS   (V)

In a food processor, blend together the tahini, garlic and lemon juice until very creamy and smooth, scraping down the sides of the processor as necessary.

Add the basil, parsley, 2 Tbsp olive oil and salt. Process for about 1 minute, again scraping down the sides as necessary.

Add half of the chickpeas and process for 1 minute. Add the remaining chickpeas and process for another 1 to 2 minutes. Add 1 to 2 tsp of water as needed to achieve an ultra-smooth, creamy texture.

Scoop the hummus into a bowl and drizzle with the remaining 1 tsp olive oil.

Keep in an airtight container in the fridge for up to 7 days.

3 Tbsp tahini

1 clove garlic, minced

1 Tbsp lemon juice

1½ cups fresh basil, chopped

½ cup fresh flat-leaf parsley, chopped

2 Tbsp extra virgin olive oil, plus 1 tsp for drizzling

1 tsp flaked sea salt

1 cup canned chickpeas, rinsed, drained and skins removed (see note, page 146)

WHIPPED CHÈVRE DIP

(PICNIC IN THE PARK , PAGE 43) — MAKES 1 ½ CUPS

Combine the chèvre, cream cheese, lemon juice and cream in a food processor and process until fluffy and smooth, 2 to 3 minutes.

Transfer to a bowl and fold in the parsley.

You can serve this immediately or keep it in an airtight container in the fridge for up to 7 days.

1 (8 oz) package chèvre

½ cup full-fat cream cheese, room temperature

2 Tbsp lemon juice

1 tsp heavy (35%) cream

2 Tbsp finely chopped fresh flat-leaf parsley leaves

ROMESCO SAUCE

(BARCELONA ON A BOARD , PAGE 115) — MAKES 2 CUPS (V)

2 slices white sandwich bread, crusts on, toasted and torn into bite-size pieces

½ cup toasted whole almonds

1 Tbsp smoked paprika

1 tsp flaked sea salt

1 tsp granulated sugar

2 large jarred roasted red bell peppers, drained

2 cloves garlic, chopped

1 large beefsteak tomato, quartered, or 2 Roma, halved

1 tsp tomato paste

¼ cup extra virgin olive oil

1 Tbsp white vinegar

To a food processor, add the toast pieces, almonds, paprika, salt and sugar and pulse until you have a crumb mixture. Pour the crumb mixture into a medium bowl.

Place the bell peppers, garlic, tomato, tomato paste, olive oil and vinegar in the food processor and blend until fairly smooth.

Empty the pepper-tomato mixture into a medium bowl. Stir in the crumb mixture a spoonful at a time until it reaches your desired consistency. A thicker consistency (more crumbs in the mixture) makes a great dip, and a thinner consistency (fewer crumbs in the mixture) makes for a great pasta sauce or a basting sauce for chicken or shrimp.

Keep in an airtight container in the fridge for up to 1 week or in the freezer for up to 3 months.

PEA PESTO

(CROSTINI FOR A CROWD , PAGE 47) — MAKES 2 CUPS (V)

1 cup frozen sweet green peas, thawed

1 small clove garlic, minced

½ cup fresh basil leaves

½ cup grated Parmesan cheese

1 Tbsp lemon juice

1 tsp flaked sea salt

½ tsp coarse ground black pepper

¼ cup (or less) extra virgin olive oil

1 tsp lemon zest, plus additional for garnish

Place the peas, garlic, basil, Parmesan, lemon juice, salt and pepper in a food processor. Pulse 10 to 12 times until well combined.

With the processor running, slowly drizzle the olive oil into the pesto until you reach a smooth consistency. You may not need all of the oil.

Transfer to a small bowl and stir in 1 tsp lemon zest. Garnish with a sprinkling of lemon zest.

Keep in an airtight container in the fridge for up to 7 days.

Romesco Sauce, Whipped Chèvre Dip (p. 149), & Pea Pesto

WASABI EDAMAME DIP

(SUSHI & SAKE , PAGE 133) — MAKES 1 CUP (V)

1 ¼ cups frozen shelled edamame
   beans
2 tsp ponzu sauce
1 tsp mirin
1 tsp garlic powder
1 tsp wasabi paste

Bring a medium pot of water to a boil over high heat. Add the frozen edamame beans, and once water comes back up to a boil, cook the beans for about 3 minutes. Drain the beans but reserve the bean water.

Place the cooked edamame beans, ponzu, mirin, garlic powder and wasabi paste in a food processor. Process until smooth, gradually adding bean water about 1 Tbsp at a time if needed, while the machine is running, until the dip is smooth and creamy.

Keep in an airtight container in the fridge for up to 3 days.

SUNSHINE MINT RAITA

(CHAAT & CHUTNEY , PAGE 128) — MAKES 1 ¾ CUPS (V)

½ English cucumber
¼ tsp flaked sea salt
1 cup full-fat plain Greek-style
   yogurt
½ cup chopped mint
1 tsp minced fresh ginger
½ tsp ground turmeric
¼ tsp ground cumin
¼ tsp ground coriander

Cut the cucumber in half lengthwise and run your spoon down the center to remove the seeds. This is where most of the liquid is stored, so if you skip this step your raita may be very loose. Using a box grater, grate the cucumber into a fine-mesh sieve placed over a medium-size bowl. Sprinkle with the salt and let some of the remaining liquids drip out.

While the cucumber drains, mix together the yogurt, mint, ginger, turmeric, cumin and coriander.

Press the cucumber against the sieve to release any remaining water, then fold into the yogurt mixture.

Cover tightly and refrigerate for at least 1 hour before serving.

Keep in the fridge in an airtight container for up to 1 week.

SMOKED TROUT DIP

(UNDER THE SEA , PAGE 49) — MAKES 2 CUPS

In a medium bowl, combine the cream cheese, mayonnaise, scallions, dill and lemon juice.

Gently fold in the flaked trout.

Keep in an airtight container in the fridge for up to 5 days.

½ cup full-fat cream cheese, room temperature
¼ cup full-fat mayonnaise
¼ cup chopped scallions
1 tsp dried dill
1 tsp lemon juice
1 cup flaked smoked trout

SEAFOOD COCKTAIL SAUCE

(UNDER THE SEA , PAGE 49) — MAKES ½ CUP   (V)

Whisk together all the ingredients in a small bowl.

Cover and let stand in the fridge for 1 hour to allow flavors to meld.

Keep in an airtight container in the fridge for up to 7 days.

½ cup ketchup
2 Tbsp jarred horseradish
1 Tbsp lemon juice
½ tsp Worcestershire sauce

Mint Green Chutney (p. 156), Red Kashmir Chutney (p. 156),
& Spicy Thai Relish

Relishes & Jams

SPICY THAI RELISH OVER CREAMY YOGURT

(WORLD FLAVORS, PAGE 135) — MAKES 2 CUPS

Finely chop the chilies, garlic, bell peppers and scallion. Mix together in a small bowl.

Add the avocado oil, fish sauce, lime juice and sugar to the bowl. Let stand in the fridge for at least 1 hour before serving.

Combine the yogurt and sour cream in a medium-size bowl.

Gently spoon the relish mixture over the yogurt mixture. Serve with chips or crudités for dipping.

The relish and yogurt can be stored separately in airtight containers in the fridge for up to 5 days.

NOTE: Using the seeds from the chilies will intensify the heat level. It's up to you to include or discard them.

2 medium-size Thai red chilies (use or discard seeds; see note)

2 cloves garlic

1 small yellow bell pepper

1 small orange bell pepper

1 scallion, green and white parts

3 Tbsp avocado oil

1 Tbsp fish sauce

1 Tbsp lime juice

1 Tbsp granulated sugar

1 cup full-fat plain Greek-style yogurt

1 cup full-fat sour cream

RED KASHMIR CHUTNEY

(CHAAT & CHUTNEY, PAGE 128) — MAKES ½ CUP (V)

10 dried Kashmiri chilies, seeded
   (see note)
10 cloves garlic
1 Tbsp lime juice
1 Tbsp granulated sugar
1 tsp flaked sea salt

Soak the seeded dried chilies in tap-hot (not boiling) water for about 1 hour, or until soft.

Remove and discard the stems and roughly chop the chilies.

Place the chopped chilies and the remaining ingredients in a food processor. Pulse several times until almost silky-smooth. If necessary, add water, ¼ tsp at a time, to loosen the mixture.

Keep in an airtight container in the fridge for up to 14 days.

NOTE: Kashmiri chilies are available at most Asian markets.

MINT GREEN CHUTNEY

(CHAAT & CHUTNEY, PAGE 128) — MAKES ¾ CUP (V)

1 to 2 green chilies, seeded and
   roughly chopped
1 cup chopped fresh cilantro
1 cup chopped fresh mint leaves
1 tsp finely grated fresh ginger
1 Tbsp lemon juice
1 tsp ground cumin
3 Tbsp water

Place all the ingredients in a high-powered blender or small food processor. Process until smooth, adding ½ tsp water to loosen the mixture if necessary.

Cover and refrigerate for 1 hour before serving.

Store in an airtight container in the fridge for up to 1 week.

CRANBERRY MUSTARD

(CHRISTMAS DINNER ON A BOARD, PAGE 101) — MAKES ½ CUP (V)

Heat the cranberries over medium-high heat until they start to pop.

Add the mustard, honey and vinegar, turn down the heat to medium-low and simmer for 5 to 7 minutes.

Transfer the mixture to a food processor or high-powered blender and blend until completely smooth.

Keep in an airtight container in the fridge for up to 7 days.

½ cup fresh cranberries
2 Tbsp grainy mustard
1 Tbsp liquid honey
1 tsp apple cider vinegar

CHERRY CABERNET RELISH

(CHRISTMAS DINNER ON A BOARD, PAGE 101) — MAKES 1¼ CUPS (V)

Place all the ingredients in a medium-size pot. Bring to a boil over medium-high heat, then turn down the heat to medium-low. Allow to simmer, uncovered and without stirring, for about 10 minutes until the sugar has melted and the mixture has reduced by at least one third.

Transfer to a food processor and pulse the mixture briefly, 5 or 6 times. This will ensure the relish has texture.

Transfer to a container and allow to cool to room temperature, uncovered. Once cool, seal the container and place in the fridge to sit for at least 2 hours before serving.

Keep in an airtight container in the fridge for up to 2 weeks.

2 cups pitted frozen or fresh cherries
⅓ cup granulated sugar
⅓ cup Cabernet Sauvignon
1 Tbsp lemon juice
½ tsp flaked sea salt

TOMATO BACON JAM

(CROSTINI FOR A CROWD, PAGE 47) —— MAKES 1 ½ CUPS

1 lb thick-cut bacon

1 large yellow onion, chopped

1 shallot, chopped

⅓ cup granulated sugar

2 ½ cups chopped Roma tomatoes
    (5 or 6)

1 Tbsp smoked paprika

2 tsp chili powder

2 Tbsp dark balsamic vinegar

1 tsp Worcestershire sauce

Cut bacon into 1″ pieces and cook in a skillet over medium heat. Just before the bacon turns crispy, use a slotted spoon to transfer it from the pan to a paper towel–lined plate.

Leave about 2 Tbsp bacon fat in the pan and add the onions and shallots. Sprinkle with the sugar and let cook over low heat, stirring occasionally, until translucent and caramelized, about 10 minutes.

Add the tomatoes, paprika, chili powder, balsamic vinegar and Worcestershire sauce. Continue to cook on low for another 10 minutes. Add the cooked bacon and cook, stirring only once, for another 10 minutes or until the mixture becomes a thick, jam-like consistency.

Keep in an airtight container in the fridge for up to 3 weeks.

KENTUCKY BOURBON BACON JAM

(RED, WHITE & BLUE, PAGE 111) —— MAKES 1 ½ CUPS

½ lb thick-cut maple bacon, roughly
    chopped

1 cup chopped sweet white onion

2 cloves garlic, smashed

½ tsp tomato paste

¼ cup bourbon

¼ cup grade A amber maple syrup

¼ cup packed brown sugar

Place the bacon in a heavy skillet over medium-low heat and cook slowly until done but not crisp. Using a slotted spoon, remove the bacon to a paper towel–lined plate. Leave 2 Tbsp bacon fat in the skillet.

Add the onions and garlic to the skillet and cook on low heat for about 10 minutes. Add the remaining ingredients, stir until well combined and let simmer, uncovered, on low for at least 15 minutes, stirring only once. It should reduce slightly and start to have a thicker, jam-like texture.

Remove from heat and fold in the bacon.

Keep in an airtight container in the fridge for up to 2 weeks.

Tomato Bacon Jam & Kentucky Bourbon Bacon Jam

BOURBON PUMPKIN BUTTER

(THANKSGIVING FEAST, PAGE 99) — MAKES 4 CUPS

2 (each 15 oz) cans pumpkin puree
(not pumpkin pie filling)

¾ cup liquid honey

¼ cup grade A amber maple syrup

¼ cup bourbon

2 Tbsp lemon juice

1 Tbsp ground cinnamon

1 tsp flaked sea salt

1 tsp ground ginger

1 tsp ground nutmeg (or ¾ tsp
freshly grated)

¼ tsp ground cloves

Place all the ingredients in a Dutch oven or deep skillet. Bring to a boil over medium-high heat, then turn down the heat to low.

Simmer, uncovered, for at least 45 minutes or up to 1 hour, stirring occasionally. The longer it cooks, the greater it will reduce and intensify in flavor.

Keep in an airtight container in the fridge for up to 1 week. This recipe can be easily halved for smaller gatherings.

NOTE: For an alcohol-free version, use ½ tsp of almond extract in place of the bourbon.

QUICK CARROT JAM

(FALL FEAST, PAGE 79) — MAKES 2 CUPS   (V)

5 medium carrots

1 ¼ cups granulated sugar

1 Tbsp bourbon

1 Tbsp lemon juice

1 tsp lemon zest

½ tsp finely chopped fresh
rosemary

Peel the carrots and chop into ¼″ coins. Place the carrots in a pot with just enough water to cover them. Bring to a simmer over medium-high heat. Turn down the heat to medium and cook the carrots until fork-tender, about 7 minutes. Drain off the water.

While the carrots are still hot, mash them with a fork. If you prefer more texture in your jam, leave some of the carrot pieces chunky. Add the remaining ingredients. If you prefer a smooth jam, transfer to a food processor and puree.

Return to low heat for about 5 minutes to continue melting the sugar, stirring occasionally. The jam may appear a bit loose while hot, but it will set up after about 3 hours in the fridge.

Transfer to a heat-safe jar and let cool to room temperature before sealing. Keep in an airtight container in the fridge for up to 3 weeks.

Bourbon Pumpkin Butter

Mushroom Paté & Butter-dipped Radishes (p. 164)

Savory Additions

MUSHROOM PÂTÉ

(POWERED BY PLANTS, PAGE 55) — MAKES 1 CUP   (V)

Place the mushrooms, shallot and garlic in a food processor and process until finely chopped. Set aside.

Heat a 10″ cast-iron skillet over medium-low heat. Add the butter, miso paste and mustard. Once they have melted, add the chopped mushroom mixture. Cook, stirring occasionally, for 15 minutes or until the water releases. Once the water has fully cooked out, add the vinegar, thyme, parsley, red pepper flakes, salt and pepper. Cook for an additional 10 minutes, stirring occasionally. The mixture should turn quite dark. Remove from heat and let cool.

Once it's completely cooled, you can serve the pâté in a bowl as a spread. If you want to shape it like a traditional pâté, lay out a piece of plastic wrap (about 8″ × 12″). Drizzle the plastic with about 1 tsp olive oil. Scoop the pâté onto the wrap, bring up the sides to encase the pâté and roll it around to form a log. Place in the fridge for at least 4 hours or overnight to firm up and let the flavors intensify. Remove the plastic before serving.

Keep in an airtight container in the fridge for up to 3 days.

NOTE: This recipe benefits from being made a day in advance, as the mushroom flavors will intensify.

20 oz cremini mushrooms, cleaned and stems removed
1 small shallot
4 cloves garlic
½ cup + 1 Tbsp unsalted butter
1 Tbsp red miso paste
1 Tbsp stone-ground (coarse) mustard
1 Tbsp sherry vinegar
1 Tbsp fresh thyme leaves
1 Tbsp chopped fresh flat-leaf parsley leaves
1 tsp red pepper flakes
1 tsp flaked sea salt
1 tsp coarse ground black pepper
1 tsp extra virgin olive oil, if shaping the pâté

BUTTER-DIPPED RADISHES

(BAGUETTES, BRIES & BERETS, PAGE 117) — MAKES 18 RADISHES   (V)

18 radishes, any varietal, greens
    attached
½ cup high-quality unsalted butter
    (see notes)
2 to 3 Tbsp high-quality large-flaked
    sea salt (see notes)

Remove the radish tops if desired, or leave them on for a fuller look. Wash and dry the radishes, lay them out on a small baking sheet or Silpat and refrigerate for 15 minutes.

Remove the radishes from the fridge and ensure they're absolutely dry.

Temper the butter. The easiest way to temper butter is to place it in a microwave-safe bowl and heat it on high in 20-second increments. Every 20 seconds, remove the butter and give it a stir. The butter should be almost half-way melted so that when you stir it, the very melted portion and the more solid portion come together to form a milky cream appearance.

Gently dip three-quarters of a dry radish half into the butter, then lay it on a dry Silpat or piece of parchment. Sprinkle the radish with a pinch of flaked sea salt so it sticks to the melted butter. Repeat this process with all of the radishes.

Transfer the radishes to the fridge, uncovered, to solidify. Serve with a side of flaked sea salt for dipping.

Keep in an airtight container in the fridge for up to 3 days.

NOTES: There are only 3 ingredients in this recipe, and the quality of all 3 will make a significant difference to the outcome. I recommend using very fresh radishes that are not soft when gently squeezed. The butter should be a high-fat, European-style butter. Don't even think about using table salt. Quality large-flaked sea salt is non-negotiable for this.

SPICY COLD TOFU

(LUNAR NEW YEAR FEAST, PAGE 131) — MAKES 1 ½ CUPS (V)

Slice the tofu into slightly larger than bite-size cubes. Place in a medium-size resealable plastic bag.

In a small dish, whisk together the garlic, bean paste, soy sauce, agave and sesame oil. Pour the mixture over the tofu, cover and let marinate in the fridge for at least 4 hours.

Top with chopped scallions and beansprouts and serve cold.

The tofu is best consumed within 24 hours.

NOTE: *Doubanjiang* is available at most Asian grocery stores. You can substitute it with the same volume of black bean sauce.

1 (12 oz) package semifirm or firm tofu
2 cloves garlic, minced
1 Tbsp *doubanjiang* (spicy bean paste; see note)
1 Tbsp soy sauce
1 tsp agave nectar
1 tsp toasted sesame oil
¼ cup chopped scallions
¼ cup beansprouts

HIYAYAKKO TOFU

(SUSHI & SAKE, PAGE 133) — MAKES 1 ½ CUPS (V)

Place the soft tofu block in a shallow serving dish just large enough to hold it.

Mix the soy and ponzu sauces together in a small bowl, then pour the mixture over the tofu.

Just before serving, top the tofu with the ginger, bonito flakes, sesame seeds, minced seaweed and scallions, in this order.

The tofu is best served immediately and should be consumed within 12 hours.

NOTE: For the sesame seeds in this recipe, I like to use either all white or a mix of black and white.

1 (14 oz package) silken (soft) tofu
3 Tbsp soy sauce
2 Tbsp ponzu sauce
½ tsp grated ginger
2 Tbsp bonito flakes
1 Tbsp sesame seeds (see note)
1 Tbsp minced seaweed
1 scallion, green and white parts, thinly sliced

VERTICAL DEVILED EGGS

(HOPPY EASTER, PAGE 91) — MAKES 12 EGGS (V)

12 extra-large eggs

¼ cup crème fraîche

2 Tbsp full-fat mayonnaise

2 tsp Dijon mustard

1 tsp sweet paprika

½ tsp flaked sea salt

Sweet paprika and fresh chives,
    for garnish (optional)

Hard-boil the eggs. Drain the eggs and rinse under cold water. Carefully peel the eggs. Sometimes sliding a small spoon under the shell will help remove the stubborn ones. Slice a very small piece of the white off the bottom of each egg so they stand up. Slice about a quarter to a third off the top of each egg so you have just a large enough hole to slide a small spoon into. Carefully remove the yolks (I find using the handle of a teaspoon works).

Place the yolks and trimmed whites into a food processor with the crème fraîche, mayonnaise, mustard, paprika and salt. Puree until smooth.

Use a spatula to scoop the filling into a medium-size piping bag with a small round tip or into a medium-size resealable plastic bag. (If using a plastic bag, first press out any air and then snip a small hole in the corner.) Pipe the filling into each standing egg white.

Garnish with a sprinkle of paprika and some fresh chives (if using).

Keep in an airtight container in the fridge for up to 3 days.

SWEET & SMOKY DEVILED EGGS

(PASSOVER BOARD, PAGE 93) — MAKES 12 EGGS (V)

12 extra-large eggs

2 tsp smoked paprika

1 tsp dry mustard

½ tsp flaked sea salt

⅛ tsp cayenne pepper

¼ cup crème fraîche

½ tsp liquid honey

2 Tbsp full-fat mayonnaise

Hard-boil the eggs. Drain the eggs and rinse under cold water. Carefully peel the eggs. Slice the eggs in half lengthwise and scoop out the yolks.

Place the yolks into a food processor with the remaining ingredients. Puree until smooth.

Using a spoon, scoop a small amount of filling into the empty egg white. Using a butter knife, level the filling flat with the white. Reserve any excess yolk filling as a dip or sandwich spread.

Keep in an airtight container in the fridge for up to 3 days.

Vertical Deviled Eggs

PICKLED SHALLOTS

(BRING OUT THE BAGELS, PAGE 31) — MAKES 1 CUP   (V)

3 medium shallots, peeled and
    thinly sliced
½ cup apple cider vinegar
½ cup water
1 Tbsp granulated sugar
1 tsp flaked sea salt
1 tsp black peppercorns

Place the shallots in a clean ½-pint mason jar with a tight-fitting lid. Set aside.

In a small pot over low heat, bring the vinegar, water, sugar and salt to a simmer, stirring frequently. Once the sugar and salt have completely dissolved, remove the pot from heat.

Pour the vinegar solution over the shallots, ensuring the shallots are completely covered. Add the peppercorns.

Cover with a tight-fitting lid or plastic wrap. Let stand for at least 2 hours. The shallots will soften and intensify over time.

Keep in an airtight container in the fridge for up to 2 weeks.

QUICK PICKLED ONIONS

(UNDER THE SEA, PAGE 49; HAPPY NEW YEAR, PAGE 105) — MAKES 1 ½ CUPS   (V)

1 medium red onion
¾ cup white vinegar
¼ cup water
1 Tbsp granulated sugar
1 tsp flaked sea salt

Using a sharp knife or mandoline, finely slice the red onion. Place the onions in a clean ½-pint mason jar.

Add the vinegar, water, sugar and salt. Seal the lid tightly and shake the jar vigorously for 1 minute.

Place in the fridge for at least 4 hours before eating.

Keep in an airtight container in the fridge for up to 2 weeks.

Pickled Shallots & Quick Pickled Onions

PICKLED CRANBERRIES

(WINTER FONDUE, PAGE 81; THANKSGIVING FEAST, PAGE 99) — MAKES 1 CUP   (V)

1 cup fresh cranberries (or thawed frozen ones)

¾ cup white vinegar

2 Tbsp granulated sugar

⅛ tsp freshly ground cinnamon or nutmeg (optional)

Fill an 8 oz mason jar with the cranberries.

Add the vinegar, sugar and cinnamon or nutmeg (if using).

Close the lid tightly, shake to combine and store the jar upside down in the fridge. The cranberries will be ready to eat within 6 hours.

Keep in an airtight container in the fridge for up to 7 days.

NOTE: Don't add *both* cinnamon and nutmeg, as that would be overpowering. For more of a pickle flavor, you can pierce the cranberries before adding them to the jar. I prefer the pop they have when left untouched, but it's a personal choice.

CAVIAR OF THE SOUTH

(RED, WHITE & BLUE, PAGE 111) — MAKES 3 CUPS   (V)

2 cups grated aged Cheddar

1 cup full-fat cream cheese, room temperature

½ cup full-fat mayonnaise

⅔ cup drained jarred pimentos

1 tsp onion powder

½ tsp garlic powder

Place all the ingredients in a large bowl and vigorously combine with a wooden spoon until creamy.

Keep in an airtight container in the fridge for up to 7 days. This recipe can be easily halved for smaller gatherings.

CASHEW RICOTTA CHEESE

(VEGAN VIBES, PAGE 58) — MAKES 1 CUP   (V)

Place the cashews in a bowl and cover with boiling water. Let soak for 1 hour.

Drain the cashews, then place them in a food processor with the remaining ingredients. Process until smooth. You may occasionally need to scrape down the sides of the processor.

Scoop the ricotta into an airtight container and place in the fridge for about 1 hour to set up before serving.

Keep in an airtight container in the fridge for up to 1 week.

1½ cups raw, unsalted whole cashews
1 Tbsp lemon juice
½ tsp onion powder
¼ tsp garlic powder
½ tsp flaked sea salt
½ tsp coarse ground black pepper

WHIPPED FETA

(CROSTINI FOR A CROWD, PAGE 47; SAY HELLO TO SUNSHINE, PAGE 73) — MAKES 1 ⅓ CUPS   (V)

Place all the ingredients in a food processor and process until smooth and fluffy.

Keep in an airtight container in the fridge for up to 1 week.

1 cup crumbled and drained feta
⅓ cup full-fat cream cheese, room temperature
1 tsp lemon juice

Chocolate Salami

Sweet Extras

CHOCOLATE SALAMI

(CHOCOLATE CHARCUTERIE DESSERT BOARD, PAGE 65) — MAKES 2 (10″) LOGS (V)

Add 2″ of water to a medium-size pot and bring to an active simmer over high heat. Place a heat-safe bowl on top of the pot, ensuring the bowl does not touch the water, and turn down the heat to medium. Add the chocolate and butter. Stir gently until melted.

In a separate medium-size bowl, mix together the sugar, egg, egg yolk, vanilla and rum. Add to the melted chocolate and continue to cook, stirring constantly, until the mixture is smooth and shiny, about 4 minutes. Remove from heat.

Add the nuts and crushed cookies and gently fold in with a spatula until well combined.

Divide the mixture onto 2 pieces of parchment paper. Roll into a log shape of your desired circumference and length (3″ × 10″ works well). Twist the ends of the parchment tightly and place in the fridge overnight or in the freezer for 4 hours.

Pour the icing sugar into a shallow bowl large enough to hold 1 log. Unwrap the chocolate logs and gently roll them one by one in the icing sugar. At this point, the logs can be served or tied with kitchen twine to resemble a dried salami.

Keep the logs in an airtight container in the fridge for up to 7 days or in the freezer for 3 months.

1½ cups finely chopped dark
    chocolate (at least 60%)
½ cup unsalted butter
½ cup granulated sugar
1 large egg
1 large egg yolk
1 tsp pure vanilla extract
2 Tbsp dark rum
2 cups mixed nuts, toasted and
    roughly chopped
1¾ cups roughly crushed ladyfinger
    cookies, about 12
⅓ cup icing sugar

NOTES: You could replace the crushed ladyfingers with the same volume of other fillings such as marshmallows, candied ginger, dried fruit, graham crackers or digestive cookies. Just remember to crush or finely chop these alternatives. If you'd rather not use rum, you can use an additional 1 Tbsp vanilla extract instead.

GOLDEN BACON POPCORN

(AND THE AWARD GOES TO, PAGE 88) — MAKES 8 CUPS

6 slices thick-cut bacon

½ cup white popping corn

Smoked flaked sea salt

30 (each ½″ × ½″) pieces edible gold leaf

In a heavy skillet on low heat, slowly cook the bacon for about 15 minutes or until fully cooked but not crisp. You want to maintain some chew to the bacon.

Transfer the bacon to a paper towel–lined plate. Reserve the bacon fat.

Place 2 Tbsp reserved bacon fat and the popping corn in a stovetop popper or heavy-bottomed pan. (If you don't have enough fat for 2 Tbsp, make up the difference with melted unsalted butter.)

Over low heat, pop the corn while continuously shaking the pot or turning the handle on the popper to keep the kernels moving. Keep the pot over low heat until you hear at least 3 to 4 seconds between pops. Remove from the heat.

Chop the bacon into bite-size pieces and add to the popcorn. Toss with salt until well combined.

Pour into a serving dish.

Sprinkle the gold leaf sparingly over the top of the popcorn for a golden effect.

NOTES: Edible gold leaf is readily available in specialty kitchen stores and online. This recipe doesn't call for butter on the cooked popcorn, but feel free to add it. I recommend using unsalted butter due to the salt content of the bacon fat.

Golden Bacon Popcorn & Chocolate-Dipped
Golden Potato Chips (p. 176)

CHOCOLATE-DIPPED GOLDEN POTATO CHIPS

(AND THE AWARD GOES TO, PAGE 88) —— MAKES ENOUGH FOR 8 SERVINGS   (V)

24 oz dark chocolate wafers

1 (16 oz) bag salted ripple potato
   chips, thick-cut or kettle style

2 tsp edible gold stars

Lay paper towel or parchment under a cooling rack.

Place the chocolate wafers in a microwave-safe bowl. In 30-second intervals, microwave the chocolate on high, stirring well between each round until the chocolate is fully melted. Do not overcook. Even if some of the chocolate does not appear to be fully melted, a few strong folds with a spatula will help combine it.

Dip individual chips halfway into the bowl of melted chocolate and place on the cooling rack. Sprinkle with a few edible gold stars. I do about 4 to 5 chips at a time. Just be sure to sprinkle the gold stars before the chocolate hardens.

Let the chocolate harden, then store in an airtight container or plastic bag for a maximum of 18 hours. The chips tend to soften over time.

QUICK & SIMPLE CHOCOLATE PUDDING

(SOMETHING SWEET, PAGE 63) —— MAKES 2 CUPS   (V)

⅓ cup unsweetened Dutch-process
   cocoa

½ cup granulated sugar

3 Tbsp cornstarch

2 cups whole milk

1 tsp pure vanilla extract

NOTE: Reduced-fat milk won't produce the same results, so be sure to use whole milk for this.

Place the cocoa, sugar and cornstarch in a medium-size pot. Stir to combine.

Place the pot over medium-high heat and gradually add the milk, about ½ cup at a time, whisking constantly.

Continue stirring until the pudding starts to bubble and thickens to a consistency similar to a thick yogurt.

Remove from heat, transfer to a bowl and stir in the vanilla.

Cover tightly with plastic wrap, letting the plastic touch the pudding to prevent a skin from forming, and refrigerate for 2 hours before serving.

Keep in an airtight container in the fridge for up to 3 days.

Quick & Simple Chocolate Pudding, Peanut Butter Fluff Dip (p. 178)
& Sweet Cream Dip (p. 178)

SWEET CREAM DIP

(FRUIT & CHEESE BOARD, PAGE 51) —— MAKES 1 ½ CUPS (V)

1 cup full-fat cream cheese, room
    temperature
½ cup full-fat vanilla Greek-style
    yogurt
1 Tbsp liquid honey

Place all the ingredients in a bowl. Using a hand mixer on medium speed, beat until combined.

Transfer to a small bowl and chill for at least 1 hour before serving.

Keep in an airtight container in the fridge for up to 3 days.

PEANUT BUTTER FLUFF DIP

(PLAYFUL PLAYDATE PLATTER, PAGE 39) —— MAKES 1 ¼ CUPS (V)

¼ cup natural smooth peanut
    butter
1 cup full-fat vanilla Greek-style
    yogurt
1 Tbsp agave nectar

Place all the ingredients in a medium-size bowl. Using a hand mixer on medium speed, beat until creamy and smooth.

Keep in an airtight container in the fridge for up to 7 days.

NOTES: If you use plain yogurt, you may want to increase the sweetener to 2 Tbsp. If you use sweetened peanut butter, you may want to reduce the agave or omit it entirely.

Other flavor options to try: use honey–flavored Greek-style yogurt and replace the agave nectar with honey for a peanut butter honey fluff; replace the agave nectar with 2 Tbsp maple syrup for peanut butter maple fluff; use nut butters like almond or cashew instead of peanut butter; or, for a nut-free dip, replace the peanut butter with sunflower seed butter.

WINE-SOAKED BLACKBERRIES

(BAGUETTES, BRIES & BERETS, PAGE 117) — MAKES 1 CUP   (V)

Place the blackberries in a small shallow bowl. Sprinkle them with the sugar and gently toss until well covered.

Add the wine, cover the bowl and place the berries in the fridge to soak for 30 minutes or up to 6 hours.

Drain and spoon over Brie or Camembert or serve in a small jar alongside a cheese board.

Keep in an airtight container in the fridge for up to 2 days.

1 cup fresh blackberries, washed and dried
2 tsp granulated sugar
¾ cup full-bodied red wine

ROASTED APRICOT PRESERVE

(SOMETHING SWEET, PAGE 63) — MAKES 1 ½ CUPS   (V)

Preheat the oven to 350°F. Select a shallow baking dish just large enough to hold the apricot halves without overlapping, and line the dish with parchment paper.

Cut the apricots in half and remove the pits. Place the apricots cut side up in the prepared baking dish. Make sure they don't overlap. Sprinkle with the sugar.

Roast the apricots for about 1 hour, uncovered, or until the sugar has caramelized and the apricots are fork-tender.

While the apricots are still hot, transfer them to a bowl and add the lemon juice, vanilla and salt. Using a fork, mash and stir the apricots until you reach the desired consistency. You should be able to spoon a small amount but still have some chunks of apricot.

Keep in an airtight container in the fridge for up to 3 weeks.

15 fresh apricots, rinsed and dried
¼ cup granulated sugar
2 Tbsp lemon juice
1 tsp pure vanilla extract
Pinch of flaked sea salt

Thank You

With heartfelt gratitude:

To Robert and everyone at Appetite by Random House, thank you for taking a chance on an ex-banker with an equal affinity for spreadsheets and cheese. You understood my vision immediately and I am forever grateful.

To my editor, Lindsay, and her team (including Lesley, Lana and Lindsay #2!), thank you for making my words better, brighter and more beautiful than I ever could on my own. You made the process so positive and encouraging. And Jennifer, you took the words and pictures and designed the book of my dreams, thank you!

To my agent, Jesse, your expertise, guidance and thoughtful answers to my thousand naive questions were so valuable. I am excited to take the next steps on this journey together.

To Janis Nicolay, thank you so much for contributing to the book. You are a true artist with incredible vision for capturing the moment perfectly.

Thank you to the Penno family and Jorge family for opening up your beautiful homes for some of my photo shoots and being such supporters of the project.

To Melissa and Ethan, where do I start? From sitting me next to Robert at my first Food Bloggers of Canada dinner, to pushing me to create through the opportunities you considered me for—this book would not have happened without you and FBC. You two have created an incredible community that I would never have found on my own. I am so very grateful our paths crossed. The work you do with FBC is raising the bar on what food blogging in Canada looks like.

One of the things I have come to truly value and appreciate over the years is my group of girlfriends. I am so very blessed to have a tribe of smart, intelligent and loyal women in my life—a combination of some who have been around since elementary school and some whom I met in the last few years. They are honest and supportive, and have been my testers, editors and biggest fans. Each one plays a unique role in my life and holds a permanent spot in my heart. Thank you for sharing your kitchens, your palates, your boards, your ideas and, above all, your positive encouragement and belief in me as a mom and an aspiring author. Every woman should be so lucky to have a tribe like mine.

Mom, Dad and Carey, you guys have been my consistent support system. Every newspaper clipping and recipe you tested made this book better, Mom. Nobody cuts and measures a board or

backdrop better than you, Dad. And dear sister, I can always count on you for the most honest feedback and loudest cheers from the stands. You three have brought me inspiration and determination and it has never gone unnoticed. Thank you for taking such good care of me and being the foundation in my life.

The little love of my life, Matteo. Everything I do is for you. When you came along, I knew whatever the next phase in life brought me, I had to put you first. I love that you eagerly tested and tasted all the recipes and were so patient when Mom said, "Not until I shoot it first." You are my heart and soul, little buddy. I'm so proud to be your mom.

And to my husband, Rick, my charcuterie eater, dip tester, board washer, tech support and all around biggest fan. Thank you for always believing I could write this book and for always telling me to do whatever makes me happy. Thank you for putting up with a year and a half of dirty dishes and meat and cheese for dinner more often than socially acceptable. I love that you love everything I make, and never complain when I bring home another board. Thank you for stepping up so I could work and write in between the moments of our family time. You have created such a beautiful life for us. I love you. ■

INDEX

Note: A **bold** page number indicates that the ingredient is in a recipe title.